LET THE EARTH TEACH YOU TORAH

ELLEN BERNSTEIN DAN FINK

SHOMREI ADAMAH שומרי אדמה KEEPERS OF THE EARTH

The mission of *Shomrei Adamah*, Keepers of the Earth, is to cultivate an awareness of nature, a practice of stewardship, and a sense of Jewish identity by engaging traditional Jewish wisdom and spirituality.

Additional copies of this book and other *Shomrei Adamah* publications may be ordered from: **Shomrei Adamah**
5500 Wissahickon Avenue #804C
Philadelphia, PA 19144
(215) 844-8150

Cover design by Josh Meyer.
Mosaic from the Synagogue at Bet Alpha, Israel, c. 500 C.E.

Printed in the United States of America.

All translations are original unless otherwise noted.

Grateful acknowledgement is made to the following publishing companies for permission to reprint copyrighted material:
Ballantine Books, Bantam Books, Charles Scribner's Sons, Earthworks Press, Ecosystems Ltd., Farrar, Straus and Giroux, Fawcett Publications, Feldheim Press, Harcourt Brace Jovanovich, HarperCollins, Hebrew Publishing Company, Jewish Publication Society, MacMillan, Melody Trails, Oxford University Press, Pantheon Books, Point Foundation, Shambhala, Soncino Press, Special Rider Music, The Burning Bush Press, The Viking Press, UAHC Press, University of Nebraska Press, Vintage Books, Yale University Press.

Please refer to pages 183-184 for full copyright citations.

ISBN 0-9632848-1-9

Text paper is recycled 50# Phoenix Opaque Natural.
Cover paper is recycled 10 pt. Envirocoat.
Printed with soy ink.
Printing by Edwards Brothers Inc.
Book design and layout by Schaffzin & Schaffzin.

You need only ask

the beasts

and they will teach you,

the birds of the sky

they will tell you,

or speak with the earth

it will teach you,

the fish of the sea

will tell you stories

—Job 12:7-8

ואולם שאל נא

בהמות

ותורך

ועוף השמים

ויגד לך

או שיח לארץ

ותורך

ויספרו לך

דגי הים

—איוב י"ב: ז-ח

For our friends and families

And for Daniel Kamesar
May his memory be for a blessing

יהא זכרו ברוך

Acknowledgements

Many people reviewed or pilot tested this work and offered helpful suggestions. Thank you to David Abram, Rabbi Dan Alexander, Rabbi Devora Bartnoff, Henya Bergman, Gordon Fuller, Rabbi Everett Gendler, Judy Hoffman, Dr. Barry Holtz, Rabbi Sam Joseph, Rabbi Gerald Kane, Rabbi Scott Kravitz, Deborah Newbrun, Bobby Orman, Dr. Edy Rausch, Rabbi Jeff Schein, Joan Schoenfeld, Rabbi Barry L. Schwartz, Neal Seldman, Rabbi Marjorie Slome, Rabbi Steve Shaw, Chris Taranta, and Miriam Wyman.

Thanks to Margo Azen, Eileen Abrams, Joe Blair, Jeffrey Dekro, Rick Lederman, and Barbara Spector for reading the manuscript and making practical recommendations. Thank you to Rabbi Gershon Winkler for researching sources. Thank you to Rabbi David Stein for *A Garden of Choice Fruit*.

Thank you to Helen Nakdimen for translations. Thank you to Liz Greenwood for fish and turtles.

Special thanks to Matt Biers, Susan Mack, and Heidi Wehmeyer. Matt contributed the "Design A Community" chapter and several of the *Bal Tashchit* materials. Susan provided some of the holiday activities. Heidi wrote several hands-on exercises.

Special thanks to Jonathan Schorsch for researching and preparing *The Opinionated Guide to Environmental Resources*. His comprehensive and entertaining descriptions bring the organizations and books he reviewed to life.

Four foundations contributed financial support to this project. A warm thank you to the Children of the Lyn and Harvey Myerhoff Foundation, the Blaustein Fund, the Scheuer Foundation and the Shefa Fund.

This project grew out of the work of *Shomrei Adamah* and it could not have happened without the support of the organization. Thanks to our members, congregations, rabbis and the *Shomrei Adamah* staff: Susan Mack and Faye Bass. I am indebted to the Nathan Cummings Foundation, the Covenant Foundation, the Educational Foundation of America, the Levinson Foundation, the Everett Foundation, the Lazar Foundation, and the Surdna Foundation whose contributions have given *Shomrei Adamah* life and paved the way for this book.

This project would not have been possible without the encouragement of several people who have believed in me and *Shomrei Adamah* since the beginning. A heartfelt thank you to Sharon Bloome, James Cummings, Eli Evans, Rabbi Joe Glaser, John Hunting, Bill Lazar, Linda and Carl Levinson, Rabbi Mordechai Liebling, Jeanne Morency, and Steven Rockefeller.

Dr. Gabriel Goldman, Director of Curriculum at the Cleveland Bureau of Jewish Education, gave hours of invaluable guidance and encouragement to this project. Without his mentorship, enthusiasm, gentle and thorough critique, this book would never have seen the light of day.

Finally, a very special thanks from Dan to Laura Rappaport and Tanya; and I owe a special debt of gratitude to Stephen Schaffzin, Eliezra Schaffzin and Rachel Brodie. Stephen designed this book and Ellie edited it. I am sure that Rachel was heaven-sent to attend to every final detail and decision from editing to translation. They all worked tirelessly through many "wee" hours to accomodate inflexible deadlines.

I am deeply touched by the contributions that these friends made to this work.
—E.B.

Contents

Introduction

When the natural world is traumatized by the tears in the web of life, when the links within societal and cultural systems are severed, things fall apart.

In the Jewish idiom, this brokenness is referred to as *shvirat ha keylim*, shattering of the vessel. In the beginning the world was one whole vessel. Then the vessel shattered into millions of pieces. It is our task *l'taken* (to fix) the vessel. This book is part of such a *tikkun* (an act of fixing). It is an attempt to bring a sense of beauty to the study of the natural world and Jewish texts. It is the product of a dream in which science, religion, ethics, politics and history are bound up into one, just as all the creatures and elements are bound up into one. It is an effort to make a whole of parts that have too long been separated.

This book is also a personal repair. I began my own *tikkun* in high school: my inner life was nourished with the wisdom of the spiritual traditions; I was immersed in the study of the relations of the Ashuelot River ecosystem; and I lived in what I thought was the most beautiful spot on earth. Dan began his *tikkun* with Shabbat walks with his father, Rabbi Arnold Fink in the woods near Washington, D.C. (Dan is number 12 in a continuous line of rabbis!). The journey from there, like all journeys, was difficult and long, replete with side trails, wrong turns, dead ends. Whenever we chose the easy way rather than our hearts' way, we were deterred in the journey, thrown off course for years at a time. With the guidance of our teachers and friends and nurtured by the wild places: the Appalachian Trail, the Colorado and Klamath Rivers, the Wissahickon River valley, we have understood some and mended some. Now with gratitude, we are passing on what we have learned about nature and about Judaism to you.

We are also passing our learning on to those who have blamed western religions for the environmental crisis, arguing that Genesis 1:26 gives humans a mandate to control nature. We believe that such an analysis is misguided.

It is not Genesis that is at fault. Genesis does not tell us what to do. Rather, it describes the human condition, the human tendency toward arrogance. When we use our gifts of power and mastery intelligently, when we apply them in the right amount and temper them with humility, we have the capacity to make the world a better place. When we exploit our gifts, when we act as if the world exists only for our personal gain, when we build Towers of Babel to science and technology, we are destroying our home and the possibilities for our future. Genesis presents us with the paradox of being human: the ability to master and the need for restraint. It is up to each one of us to resolve this tension within ourselves.

At the heart of the environmental crisis is a skewed relationship between humans and the material world. And at the heart of Judaism are teachings on how to live in the material world. The essence of Jewish teachings is a principle called *mikadesh hol*, making the secular sacred. It is a principle that invites us to look at the material world, really see it and then transform it. We are guided in this process by our obligation to say *brachot*, praising God for the most ordinary events of daily life, and through the laws of *kashrut* (kosher) which transform the basic necessity of eating into a sacrament. We are even encouraged to make an abstract concept like time holy by setting aside one day a week to honor God and creation.

Ultimately, everything is sacred. It is a question, then, of seeing, and acting out of respect, humility and love for God and all creation. As is implicit in the title and message of this book: *Let the Earth Teach You Torah*. Let your reverence for it guide you in all your ways.

Ellen Bernstein

Founder, Director
Shomrei Adamah

Mt. Airy
Philadelphia, Pennsylvania

June 29, 1992
28 Sivan, 5752

How To Use This Book

In its present incarnation, this text functions as a guidebook for teaching Jewish perspectives on the human relationship with nature, geared toward a broad adult and teen audience.

This guide has integrity when taken as a whole; however, it is not critical to follow chapter by chapter. Many people will pick and choose and adapt the contents to suit their needs. Our goal was to present you with the resources you will need to teach a variety of ecological concepts through a Jewish lens. It is therefore better to approach this work as a smorgasbord to choose from rather than an exact recipe to follow.

Each chapter begins with a background section for the leader. Objectives for each chapter are identified and materials are presented at the outset. If you are teaching this book as a course, be sure to read ahead each week to the "Materials and Preparation" section of the subsequent chapter. You may want to supplement individual participation by asking participants to bring newspaper articles or other materials to each meeting. This course encourages group participation wherever possible; we would like the participants to help determine the direction the course will take. The idea is for the participants to ultimately take over the course with the leader simply facilitating.

Each chapter consists of activities and text study. The texts for study, along with questions and answer sheets, are found at the back of each chapter. There are separate worksheets for the leader and the participants. You can photocopy the "Readings & Worksheets" to use as handouts, but we ask that you please respect copyright laws regarding the rest of this book.

There was an overwhelming request from our readers to provide time estimates for each activity; we've tried to address this need by creating a system of symbols that indicate the approximate length of time needed to complete various activities:

▲ = 5-10 minutes

▲▲ = 10-20 minutes

▲▲▲ = more than 20 minutes

Originally the work was designed as an 11-unit course, each unit requiring roughly 50 minutes to complete. We soon realized that while there is more than 50 minutes' worth of material in each unit, the timing will, obviously, depend on the number of participants and the level of enthusiasm for each activity. We encourage you to take the time you and the participants need. You may occasionally wish to take two full meetings to cover one unit or you may want to take a full period to do a close reading of one text while omitting other pieces in any given unit. Please experiment and let us know what works for you. We are eager to make improvements based on the experiences you have using this book.

Most readings and activities are designed for adults and older teens (age 15 and up). You may find, however, that some of the texts are too difficult for high school students (Martin Buber, Annie Dillard). You might assign more difficult texts for students to take home and read with their families, or as special projects. With a little creativity, much of the contents can also be adapted for younger students.

Try to take a look at the supplementary activities in advance. They are located in the addendum and if you want to do any of them you will need to determine where you might want to fit them in. Take special note of the garden project. If you embark on this project, you will probably want to start as early as possible.

Some additional things that can enrich the experience for the participants include keeping a journal of their observations both of the natural world and of their intellectual/spiritual development. You may also want to assign each participant a book to read or a film to review over the course of study. The nature-writing tradition in America runs strong and deep. It is an aspect of our heritage in which we can take great pride. In the resource section, we have included an annotated list of our favorite books that should be useful in getting people started. We've also offered (you) a selection of films that focus on environmental themes that you may want to use as a supplement to any one of the units. For additional references, each of the texts within this book is fully cited in the Bibliography. We suggest that each participant choose a selection from these lists, review it and share the message of the book or film with the rest of the group.

Similarly, the media is a fertile source of material that will enhance your studies; we suggest that both you and group members watch for newspaper articles, television specials and documentaries on environmental topics and discuss them in class when appropriate. We would also like to make the Jewish texts, terms and personalities mentioned here as accessible as possible to our readers. Hebrew words are explained in the Glossary of Hebrew and Jewish Terms.

There is a resource section toward the end of the curriculum that lists national environmental organizations and gives you a feel for each organization's work. For your convenience, we have also listed some local environmental organizations. This section will be particularly useful for the chapters on "The Human Place" and "Ecology, Judaism and *Tikkun Olam*." This resource list provides the perfect opportunity for you and participants to take what you have learned and make things happen.

One of the serious side effects of urban living and technological growth is a loss of connection with nature. We've forgotten the essential link between *adam* (earthling) and *adamah* (earth). The environmental crisis is not only a technological problem with technical and legal solutions. It is a spiritual and moral crisis. An environmental crisis occurs when an entire civilization overlooks the inherent value of air, land, soil, water and species, and approaches the natural world as a tool box of resources to use for its own gain.

If our obliviousness to the gifts of nature is the root of the environmental crisis, then the task at hand is to learn to see and appreciate nature and God's presence in all of life. In the year 1070, Rabbi Bahya Ibn Pakuda of Spain was distressed that people were so obsessed with material wealth and personal gain that they took God and nature for granted. "We must obligate ourselves to meditate on creation," he said. "Try to understand both the smallest and the greatest of God's creatures. Examine carefully those which are hidden from you" (*Duties of the Heart*, p.137). Bahya's message still holds today.

The goal of the following exercises is to show that the environmental crisis is a result of a skewed perspective and a twisted value system. The first step in becoming *shomrei adamah*, keepers of the earth, is to learn how to see and value nature. We can use Jewish teachings to guide us on our way.

OBJECTIVES

•Participants will learn to "see" more closely by opening their senses to nature's fine details.

•Participants will discuss their personal experiences of increased perception and awareness.

•Participants will explain why both Judaism and ecological concerns impel us to pay close attention to what is happening around us.

MATERIALS & PREPARATION

•Copies of Kushner (see Readings & Worksheets) and Genesis 28 for every two participants.

•Paper and writing utensils for participants. Colored pencils or crayons provide an additional dimension to the exercise.

•Natural objects, such as flowers, rocks, sticks, grass, feathers, animal hair or exoskeletons (insect shells), brought by leader and participants.

Seeing

Introduction ▲

Read aloud from the selection by Annie Dillard (See Readings & Worksheets). Dillard, author of *Pilgrim at Tinker Creek* among many other books, is known for her rapture with the day-to-day events of the natural world. Read Dillard carefully, in order to grasp her meaning. If Dillard is too difficult, see alternative selections by Richard Nelson and Natalie Goldberg (See Readings & Worksheets). Nelson is a contemporary nature writer, able to bring the natural world to life through his very careful attention to detail. Goldberg writes about the necessity of attention to detail from a writer's perspective. The following discussion questions can easily be adapted to these other readings. Attention to detail is the mark of a great writer, just as it is the mark of a *shomer(et) adamah* (a "keeper of the earth").

DISCUSSION QUESTIONS

•What are some preeminent values in American culture?
Material wealth, status, accumulation of things, technological superiority.

•What do you think this piece about seeing by Annie Dillard (or, the selections from the other authors) might have to do with ecology and the environment?
The first step in becoming shomrei adamah *is to recognize that our sight is limited; the second step is to cultivate "seeing." Seeing is a skill that can be learned, like any other skill. The environmental crisis is the result of a culture that does not value or care for nature. If nature has no face, it is easy to exploit and abuse. (Think about the similarities to war and oppression, when people do not have a face.) Abraham Joshua Heschel tells us that "man has indeed become a tool-making animal, and the world is now a gigantic tool box for the satisfaction of his needs" (God in Search of Man, p.34). When we use nature for our own needs we lose sight of its inherent value. Annie Dillard's piece teaches us how to look at nature, an ability that many of us have lost.*

•What might this piece have to do with Judaism?
One of our goals is to break free of old thought patterns that limit our "seeing" and to gain a fresh appreciation of the natural world. Judaism helps us wake up and teaches us the inherent value of all living things. For example, the very act of reciting blessings forces us to consider our actions like eating and seeing and smelling rather than just lapse into senseless and mechanistic responses to our environment. Another example is in the Mishnah (Brachot 1:2), where the various colors of the sky as the day breaks is discussed in detail.

Learning to See ▲▲▲

Attention to detail is a skill that we must practice or learn; it does not come naturally to most of us. Furthermore, when we observe, each of us notices something different. This activity is designed to teach participants to look more closely and to discover what can be learned from this kind of "seeing."

•What is the difference between looking and seeing?
"Looking at" implies a superficial stance, noticing the immediate outer qualities, but "seeing" implies more of a relationship between the two parties. "Seeing" implies knowing the details; it implies understanding.

This activity can be done indoors or outside. Outside, participants can choose a natural object from their surroundings. Indoors, participants choose from the natural objects the leader and the participant have brought in. Below is a series of questions that invite the participants into a deeper understanding of their objects; you may want to go over these questions first or write them on the blackboard. They are primarily for participants who need help getting started.

Part 1 ▲

Participants choose one object and find a quiet place to sit. They should "experience" their object as fully as possible by using all of their senses. Encourage them to write down everything they notice, passing no judgment on the thoughts that enter their minds.

Here are some sample questions to motivate the participants to think about the many ways they can experience their object:

•What does it look like? Taste like? Smell like? What colors can you see in the object? Is it solid, mottled, striped, spotted? Close your eyes and brush it against your skin. How does it feel? Does it have parts? What uses do the parts serve? What emotions (calm, happy, sad, etc.) do you feel as you explore your object? Why did you choose this object? Does it make any sounds as you play with it? What uses can you imagine (real or fanciful) for the object or its parts? What memories does it evoke? What story does it tell?

•Flower, Plant: Is the stem hairy, smooth, sticky? What about the sepals (the outer, protective leaves)? What shape are the petals, the leaves? Can you see veins in them? What is their purpose? Is there any nectar? How does it taste? How are the leaves arranged on the stem? Does it have different smells? Who or what might use this plant (insects, birds, people, etc.)? What would they use it for?

•Stick: Is the bark rough or smooth? Is the stick flexible or brittle? Has it started to decompose? What size plant do you think it came from? Are there protrusions on it? What are they from? How does the bark come off? Does it peel off in strips, or come off in chunks? What do those pieces remind you of?

•Feather: What patterns do you see in the feather? How might this feather have left the bird and come to you? What does this feather do for the bird? Does it need preening (smoothing and cleaning)? How do the filaments stay together?

•Exoskeleton: What patterns do you see? What is an exoskeleton for? Do you have one? Do you have something that serves the same purpose? Who lived inside the casing? What could the insect have eaten? What might eat the insect? Did it fly well? Can you tell why it died? How do you feel when you hold it?

Part 2 ▲

Have a few volunteers share their observations with the group. Notice what different members say about similar objects. Point out the differences. Can they imagine why they responded differently? Note that we bring ourselves and our particular worldview to everything we see and experience.

Part 3 ▲

Repeat the activity with a new object. Participants should have gained confidence from the first exercise to enable them to experience their object more fully. Encourage participants to feel free to respond in creative ways, such as through poetry, a rap, a story as told by the object, or a song.

Part 4 ▲

Discuss as a group how focusing on something familiar can change the way we feel in our surroundings, how much we notice, how much we appreciate. Have participants ever experienced anything like that on their own, a special moment when their attention was called to something they didn't usually notice, a special moment in nature? Share a few stories.

Through these activities, we've seen that when we pay close attention, we often notice things we had never been aware of, but were in front of us all along. Judaism also teaches us that we need to look closely at the world and not take things for granted.

Divide the group in half. Give one group a copy of the Kushner text. Give the other a copy of Chapter 28 of Genesis (paying particular attention to Gensis 28:16). Rabbi Lawrence Kushner is rabbi of Congregation Beth El in Sudbury, Massachusetts. He has written many books that help us see the miracles of everyday life. Each group will read its selection and make up a two minute skit to present to their classmates.

OR

Divide the group into pairs. Ask the pairs to read the two texts, cited above, aloud to each other. As they read they should be thinking about how the readings are related to the Dillard selection and the topic of Judaism and ecology.

Reconvene (after reading in pairs or skits) to discuss the texts.

DISCUSSION QUESTIONS

•Did you identify with the characters? Do you think you are more like Reuven and Shimon, who never learned to see, or Jacob, who did learn? Think of times when you discovered something "new" that had, in fact, been there all along.
Examples: finding something "right under your nose" after a long search, noticing a smell that your house has always had only after returning from a vacation, noticing a toadstool in your yard only after the baseball you've been tossing lands by it.

•If "God was there all along," why didn't Jacob perceive God from the beginning?
Perhaps he was too busy with other things, was asleep, or, like Reuven and Shimon, "wasn't looking in the right direction."

•What keeps us from noticing the world around us in the way that Reuven, Shimon and Jacob failed to see their world?
Being too busy with day-to-day matters, the dulling force of routine, assuming that there is nothing to see, being in a bad mood, etc.

•Rabbi Kushner says that "to be a Jew means to wake up and to keep your eyes open to the many beautiful, mysterious and holy things that happen all around us every day." Why is being awake an important part of Judaism?
a) Judaism may take on new meanings to us and become more relevant to our lives when we take the time to study its laws and traditions.
b) It is by cultivating our awareness that we, like Jacob, might come to experience God.

c) Looking closely reminds us of the bounty of the world beyond ourselves, and therefore may help us become less egotistical and more concerned about others. Only if we pay close attention to our world, recognizing its beauty and its problems, will we be moved to perform acts of tikkun olam (repairing the world).

•Why is "being awake"—paying close attention—important in ecological thinking?

a) Looking closely helps us appreciate the wonders of nature. Once we appreciate the diversity and value of all life and of our ecosystems, we are more likely to protect them.

b) By paying close attention, we learn how the lives of various creatures are intertwined with each other and with our own lives.

c) Looking closely helps us recognize problems that must be addressed; noticing dying trees, for example, may make us aware of the dangers of acid rain.

•Notice the similarity between the ways that Judaism and ecological concerns compel us to pay close attention to our world. Now that we know the importance of "seeing" in both Jewish and ecological thinking, how can we "wake ourselves up?"

By learning about and experiencing nature; by removing our insulated walls; by seeing, not just looking at the world around us; by recognizing that our place in the natural world as well as our Jewish moral responsibilities (implicit in the commandments) demand us to wake up.

Bringing It Home ▲

To end, have a volunteer read the following passage from Aldo Leopold's *A Sand County Almanac*. Many people consider Leopold America's first great environmentalist. He was born in 1887 and worked for the forest service much of his life. He died fighting a grass fire on a neighbor's farm.

"A March morning is only as drab as he who walks in it without a glance skyward, ear cocked for geese. I once knew an educated lady, banded by Phi Beta Kappa, who told me that she had never heard or seen the geese that twice a year proclaim the revolving seasons to her well insulated roof. Is education possibly a process of trading awareness for things of lesser worth? The goose who trades his is soon a pile of feathers."
—Aldo Leopold, *A Sand County Almanac*, p.20

Awareness is an integral part of both understanding and action. Jewish tradition tells us to be aware of our actions, and of our intentions when we act. The Hebrew word for intention is *kavannah*. By developing our own *kavannah*, we can add meaning to what we see and do. The *kavannah* for the upcoming week is to begin to pay attention to the daily miracles. Make an effort to really see one new thing. Strive to become observant of your daily environment. This kind of observance is the first step to becoming *shomrei adamah*.

Further Reading

Annie Dillard, *Pilgrim At Tinker Creek*.

Aldo Leopold, *A Sand County Almanac*.

Richard Nelson, *The Island Within*.

Robert Finch and John Elder, Ed.s; *The Norton Book of Nature Writing*.

Seeing

Introduction: From Annie Dillard, *Pilgrim at Tinker Creek*, pp. 16-18.

Reading

It is still the first week in January, and I've got great plans. I've been thinking about seeing. There are lots of things to see: unwrapped gifts and free surprises. The world is fairly studded and strewn with pennies cast broadside from a generous hand. But—and this is the point—who gets excited by a mere penny? . . . It is dire poverty indeed when a man is so malnourished and fatigued that he won't stoop to pick up a penny. But if you cultivate a healthy poverty and simplicity, so that finding a penny will literally make your day, then, since the world is in fact planted in pennies, you have with your poverty bought a lifetime of days. It is that simple. What you see is what you get.

I used to be able to see flying insects in the air. I'd look ahead and see, not the row of hemlocks across the road, but the air in front of it. My eyes would focus along that column of air, picking out flying insects. But I lost interest, I guess, for I dropped the habit. Now I can see birds. Probably some people can look at the grass at their feet and discover all the crawling creatures. I would like to know grasses and sedges—and care. Then my least journey into the world would be a field trip, a series of happy recognitions.

. . . Unfortunately, nature is very much a now-you-see-it, now-you-don't affair. A fish flashes, then dissolves in the water before my eyes like so much salt. Deer apparently ascend bodily into heaven; the brightest oriole fades into leaves. . . For nature does reveal as well as conceal: now-you-don't-see-it, now-you-do. For a week last September migrating red-winged blackbirds were feeding heavily down by the creek at the back of the house. One day I went out to investigate the racket; I walked up to a tree, an Osage orange, and a hundred birds flew away. They simply materialized out of the tree. I saw a tree, then a whisk of color, then a tree again. I walked closer and another hundred blackbirds took flight. Not a branch, not a twig budged: the birds were apparently weightless as well as invisible. Or, it was as if the leaves of the Osage orange had been freed from a spell in the form of red-winged blackbirds; they flew from the tree, caught my eye in the sky, and vanished. When I looked again at the tree the leaves had reassembled as if nothing had happened. Finally I walked directly to the trunk of the tree and a final hundred, the real diehards, appeared, spread, and vanished. How could so many hide in the tree without my seeing them? The Osage orange, unruffled, looked just as it had looked from the house, when three hundred red-winged blackbirds cried from its crown. I looked downstream where they flew, and they were gone. Searching, I couldn't spot one. I wandered downstream to force them to play their hand, but they'd crossed the creek and scattered. One show to a customer. These appearances catch at my throat; they are the free gifts, the bright coppers at the roots of trees.

It's all a matter of keeping my eyes open. Nature is like one of those line drawings of a tree that are puzzles for children: Can you find hidden in the leaves a duck, a house, a boy, a bucket, a zebra, and a boot? Specialists can find the most incredibly well-hidden things. . . The lover can see, and the knowledgeable. The point is that I just don't know what the lover knows; I just can't see the artificial obvious that those in the know construct. The herpetologist asks the native, "Are there snakes in that ravine?" "Nosir." And the herpetologist comes home with, yessir, three bags full. Are there butterflies on that mountain? Are the bluets in bloom, are there arrowheads here, or fossil shells in the shale?

Seeing

Introduction: From Richard Nelson, *The Island Within*, pp. 35-36.

Alternative Reading

The bird's placid demeanor gives rise to an idea. A gray skeleton of tree leans beneath his perch, making a ramp I can climb to get closer. His eyes fix on me as I ease to the leaning trunk's base; but he holds fast to the branch. I've never been this close to a wild, free eagle. I think of the ancient hunters, lying hidden in the loosely covered pits with bait fastened above, waiting to grab the descending talons. But I seek no blood, no torn sacred feather. Closeness is my talisman, the sharing of eyes, scents twisted together in the same eddy of wind, the soft sound of a wheezing breath, quills ticking in the breeze, feet scuttling on dry bark, and the rush of air beneath a downswept wing.

I inch slowly. . . slowly up the bare trunk, twist myself around the stubs of broken limbs, until I'm twenty feet from the bird and can't come any closer. Nothing is left except to be here—two intense, predatory animals, given to great suddenness, for these moments brought within whatever unknowable circle surrounds us. Perhaps neither of us will ever be so near another of our respective kinds again. I don't need to believe that we communicate anything more than a shared interest and regard, as we blink across the distances that separate our minds.

When the eagle moves or teeters, I can see his feet clutch the branch more tightly, and the needled tips of his talons pierce more deeply through the brittle, flaking bark into the wood beneath. Two loose, downy feathers hang incongruously from his breast, out-of-place feathers that quiver in the gentle current of air. I think how strange it is that I expect an eagle to look groomed and perfect, like the ones in books.

The bird cranes his head down to watch me, so the plumage on his neck fluffs out. His head is narrow, pinched, tightly feathered; his eyes are silver-gold, astringent, and stare forward along the curved scythe of his beak. Burned into each eye is a constructed black pupil, like the tightly stung arrow of a crossbow aimed straight toward me. What does the eagle see when he looks at me, this bird who can spot a herring's flash in the water a quarter-mile away? I suppose every stub of whisker on my face, every mole and freckle, every eyelash, the pink flesh on the edge of my eyelid, the red network of vessels on the white of my eye, the radiating colors of my iris, his own reflection on my pupil, or beneath the reflection, his inverted image on my retina. I see only the eagle's eye, but wonder if he sees down inside mine. Or inside me, perhaps.

Seeing

Introduction: From Natalie Goldberg, *Writing Down The Bones*, pp. 43-44.

Alternative Reading

"The Power of Detail"

Our lives are at once ordinary and mythical. We live and die, age beautifully or full of wrinkles. We wake in the morning, buy yellow cheese, and hope we have enough money to pay for it. At the same instant we have magnificent hearts that pump through all sorrows and all winters we are alive on earth. We are important and our lives are important, magnificent really, and their details are worthy to be recorded. This is how writers must think, this is how we must sit down with pen in hand. We were here; we are human beings; this is how we lived. Let it be known, the earth passed before us. Our details are important. Otherwise, if they are not, we can drop a bomb and it doesn't matter.

Yad Vashem, a memorial for the Holocaust, is in Jerusalem. It has a whole library that catalogues the names of the six million matyrs. Not only did the library have their names, it also had where they lived, were born, anything that could be found out about them. These people existed and they mattered. Yad Vashem as a matter of fact means "memorial to the name." It was not the nameless masses that were slaughtered; they were human beings.

. . . We have lived; our moments are important. This is what it is to be a writer: To be the carrier of details that make up history, to care about the orange booths in the coffee shop in Owatonna.

Recording the details of our lives is a stance against bombs and their mass ability to kill, against too much speed and efficiency. A writer must say yes to life, to all of life: the water glasses, the Kemp's half-and-half, the ketchup on the counter. It is not a writer's task to say, "It is dumb to live in a small town or to eat in a cafe when you can eat macrobiotic at home." Our task is to say a holy yes to the real things of our life as they exist—the real truth of who we are: several pounds overweight, the grey, cold street outside, the Christmas tinsel in the showcase, the Jewish writer in the orange booth across from her blond friend who has black children. We must become writers who accept things as they are, come to love the details, and step forward with a yes on our lips so there can be no more noes in the world, noes that invalidate life and stop the details from continuing.

Seeing

Text Study: Opening Your Eyes: From Lawrence Kushner, *The Book of Miracles*, pp. 3-6

Reading

When the people of Israel crossed through the Red Sea, they witnessed a great miracle. Some say it was the greatest miracle that ever happened. On that day they saw a sight more awesome than all the visions of the prophets combined. The sea split and the waters stood like great walls, while Israel escaped to freedom on the distant shore. Awesome. But not for everyone.

Two people, Reuven and Shimon, hurried along among the crowd crossing through the sea. They never once looked up. They noticed only that the ground under their feet was still a little muddy like a beach at low tide.

"Yucch!" said Reuven, "there's mud all over this place!"

"Blecch!" said Shimon, "I have muck all over my feet!"

"This is terrible," answered Reuven, "When we were slaves in Egypt, we had to make our bricks out of mud, just like this!"

"Yeah," said Shimon. "There's no difference between being a slave in Egypt and being free here."

And so it went, Reuven and Shimon whining and complaining all the way to freedom. For them there was no miracle. Only mud. Their eyes were closed. They might as well have been asleep. (Exodus Rabbah 24:1)

People see only what they understand, not necessarily what lies in front of them. For example, if you saw a television set, you would know what it was and how to operate it. But imagine someone who had never seen a television. To such a person it would be just a strange and useless box. Imagine being in a video store, filled with movies and stories and music, and not even knowing it. How sad when something is right before your eyes, but you are asleep to it. It is like that with our world too.

Something like this once happened to Jacob, our father. He dreamed of a ladder joining heaven and earth. Upon it angels were climbing up and down. Then God appeared and talked to Jacob. When he awoke the next morning, Jacob said to himself, "Wow! God was in this very place all along, and I didn't even know it!" (Genesis 28:16)

Rabbi Shelomo Yitzchaki, who lived in France eight hundred years ago and whom we call Rashi (after the initials of his name), explained what Jacob meant: "If I had known that God would be here, then I wouldn't have gone to sleep!"

To be a Jew means to wake up and to keep your eyes open to the many beautiful, mysterious, and holy things that happen all around us every day. Many of them are like little miracles: when we wake up and see the morning light, when we taste food and grow strong, when we learn from others and grow wise, when we hug the people we love and feel warm, when we help those around us and feel good. All these and more are there for us every day, but we must open our eyes to see them; otherwise we will be like Reuven and Shimon, able to see only mud.

Suppose, right now, your eyes are closed. How do you wake up?

In Judaism it is understood that everything was created by the Creator with a special purpose and a place. There are no excesses, no superfluity, and no waste.

"The Rabbis said: Even though you may think them superfluous in this world, creatures such as flies, bugs and gnats, have their allotted task in the scheme of creation, as it says "And God saw everything that God had made, and behold, it was very good," (Genesis1:31)."—Genesis Rabbah 10:7

The discipline of ecology (*ecos*=house, *logy*=study of) rests on the understanding that everything in nature has its place and value. The earth, its habitats and inhabitants operate as one giant living organism, each continually affecting the other. There are no excesses, no superfluity and no waste. The goal of this lesson is to awaken participants to the value and diversity of life in nature.

•Participants will understand that all life has value and that everything has a special place, both from a Jewish perspective and from an ecological perspective.

•Tape of "Turn, Turn, Turn," copies of the lyrics (see Readings & Worksheets) and audio equipment.
•A few apples, a knife.
•Copies of Genesis, copies of readings, and Participant Worksheets (see Readings & Worksheets).

Purpose and Place

Opening

Set up a record or tape player so that as participants enter, they are greeted with the song "Turn, Turn, Turn" from the Byrds' Greatest Hits album. Motion them to be seated and listen or sing along with the lyrics. You will not discuss the music; you are playing it to whet their appetites. You can give them a copy of the lyrics at the end of the session, as a memento of what they learned today. Do make sure to let them know that the source of the song is from Ecclesiastes (See Readings & Worksheets).

Useless Creatures ▲

Ask the group to list aloud all of the plants and animals they believe are bad or they think are useless. "If you could rid the world of one creature, what would it be?" (Note: Encourage the participants to be enthusiastic with their responses. Usually, they will be quick to offer examples. If not, the leader may offer a spiteful assessment of one creature, such as mosquitos, snakes, spiders or poison ivy.)

Make a list of the creatures on the blackboard, with the advocate's name next to it. Let the participants know you'll be getting back to this list at the end of the lesson.

No Waste in Nature—The Apple ▲

Adapted from Avigdor Miller's, *Rejoice O Youth,* pp. 84-86

Distribute slices of apples to everyone and keep one apple whole.

Before eating the apple, tell the group that we are going to notice everything we can about it. We're learning that there is no waste, no superfluity in nature. How does the apple demonstrate this?

Let's take a look at the "miraculous" packaging of the apple. Here is a package that advertisers would pay millions of dollars to reproduce. What is so special about the apple's packaging?

• For starters, it is a perfectly fitting package. No matter what shape the apple takes, no matter what bumps or curves the apple has, its package, the skin, is always a perfect fit with absolutely no waste. And to top it all off it's waterproof!

• Secondly, the apple's package includes a built-in color freshness indicator. As soon as an apple is ripe for eating, its package turns a bright red or green or yellow color.

• The package attracts the consumer not only through its color, but also through its smell. A ripe apple smells fresh and announces that it is ready to be consumed.

• When the apple becomes over-ripe, its stem loosens its grip on its branch and the apple eventually tumbles to the ground. What we have, then, is a perfectly fitting, waterproof package that has a built-in color indicator of freshness and emits a fragrant odor to attract the consumer.

• Furthermore, the apple's package is constructed so that bacteria and other harmful agents are prevented from getting into the fruit of the apple. Yet, the package is edibly soft. Soft enough for even the smallest caterpillar to eat through.

No less miraculous is the construction of the inside of the apple. Consider the following points:

• Apples are composed mostly of water, yet hardly a drop spills out when the apple is cut open.

• The seeds of the apple, its means of reproducing itself, are clearly meant not to be digested. They are contained in a plastic-like chamber in the center of the apple that resists chewing and contains no fruit.

• And, if seeds are ingested by birds, animals or humans, they are not digested. Seeds are coated with a covering that can withstand the powerful acids inside the digestive system. Seeds pass through with no damage and are still capable of growing another apple tree.

Text Study: A Purpose & A Place ▲▲

Divide the group up into sub-groups of 4-8 people each to study the two primary texts, Genesis 1-2:4 and the Selections from Job (See Readings & Worksheets). Each sub-group will receive one of the texts to study as well as the supplemental text sheet. Each sub-group will also receive some questions to help them think about the materials. They will read the text aloud in their group and will do their best to answer the questions. The supplemental readings may shed some light on the text study and may be of help in answering the questions. At the end of ten minutes they will regroup as a whole and one spokesperson per group will give a synopsis of their reading and of what the group learned.

POINTS TO EMPHASIZE

Each of these readings teaches that everything has a purpose and a place; everything that was created by God belongs here and, more specifically, belongs in a particular place. Furthermore, the *diversity* of creation is valuable. We may not understand the purpose of the thing, but that does not mean it does not have a purpose and a unique place in the world. What are the ramifications when you believe that something or someone does not belong? What are the ramifications when a powerful section of the population believes something does not belong on the earth? How does it make you personally feel to know you belong; how do you feel when you think people do not value you?

Defending Creation ▲

Ask a volunteer to play God and defend Creation. Take one of the animals from the "blacklist" of "useless" creatures that you created at the beginning of the lesson. The participant who put the creature on the list must prosecute the animal. God must defend the animal, stating each creature's good qualties. Move through the whole list of animals until they are all redeemed. Alternatively, you may also choose to have the leader play God. Put God on trial for creating "bad" animals. Participants play the prosecutors; God must defend the creation.

Draw some inspiration for this exercise from the *Talmud*, which teaches that by watching a cat cover up its excrement, we can learn about modesty; from the dove which mates for life, we learn about fidelity and devotion; and from an ant which never touches another ant's store of food, we learn about honesty. (Babylonian *Talmud, Erubin* 100b)

Bringing It Home ▲

In this lesson we have learned there is divine value in all of life and in the great diversity of life. We have learned this from both a Jewish and an ecological perspective.

Have a volunteer read the following interpretation of the line from Psalm 92:13, "The righteous shall flourish like the palm tree." The *kavannah* for this week is to imagine how in our human communities we can live more harmoniously with nature.

As no part of the date palm is wasted—
its dates being eaten,
its new branches used for ritual blessing
its fronds for covering a *sukkah* (ritual hut),
its fibers for ropes,
its leaves for sieves,
its trunks for rafters—
so there are none worthless among Israel;
some are versed in Bible;
others know some *Mishnah*;
some are masters of *Aggadah*; others do good deeds;
still others promote social justice.
—Numbers Rabbah 3:1

To end the unit, teach the blessing over the diverse forms of creation:

ברוך אתה ד׳ אלקינו מלך העולם משנה הבריות.

Baruch Atah Adonai, Eloheynu Melech Ha-olam, m'shaneh ha-breeyot.

Praise to You *Adonai*, our God and Universal Ruler, Who makes all varieties of creatures.

For Further Reading

Gary Paul Nabhan, *The Desert Smells Like Rain: A Naturalist in Papago Indian Country*

Purpose and Place

Opening: Song Lyrics

Readings

"Turn, Turn Turn" from *The Byrds' Greatest Hits* album is adapted from Ecclesiastes 3:1-8; the biblical text is found below the lyrics to the song.

To every thing turn turn turn

There is a season turn turn turn

And a time for every purpose under heaven

A time to be born; a time to die

A time to plant; a time to reap

A time to kill; a time to heal

A time to laugh; a time to weep

A time to build up; a time to break down

A time to dance; a time to mourn

A time to cast away stones; a time to gather stones together

A time of love; a time of hate

A time of war; a time of peace

A time you may embrace; a time to refrain from embracing

A time to gain; a time to lose

A time to rend; a time to sew

A time to love; a time to hate

A time for peace; I swear it's not too late.

Ecclesiastes 3:1-8

For everything there is a time and a season for everything desired under the heavens.

A time to birth	and a time to die.
A time to plant	and a time to uproot the planted.
A time to kill	and a time to heal.
A time to breach	and a time to build.
A time to cry	and a time to laugh.
A time for mourning	and a time for dancing.
A time to throw stones	and for gathering stones.
A time to embrace	and a time to be far from an embrace.
A time to search	and a time to let go.
A time to guard	and a time to discard.
A time to rip	and a time to mend.
A time to be silent	and a time to speak.
A time to love	and a time to hate.
A time for war	and a time for peace.

Purpose and Place

Text Study

Readings

1. Genesis 1:1 - 2:4

2. Job : (Job 38: 1-4, 12,16,18, 28, 31, 33; 39:1,19, 26; 42: 1-6)

God answered Job out of the tempest and said:
Who is this who darkens counsel, uttering words without knowledge?
Gird your loins like a man; and I will ask you and you will inform Me.
Where were you when I laid the foundations of the earth?
Speak if you have understanding.
Have you ever commanded the day to break, known the place of dawn?
Have you been brought to the depths of the sea, or walked in the recesses of the deep?
Have you surveyed the expanses of the earth? Tell Me if you know all of these.
Does the rain have a father who begot the drops of dew?
Can you tie cords to Pleiades or undo the reigns of Orion?
Do you know the laws of heaven or impose its authority on earth?
Did you know the time when mountain goats give birth?
Can you watch the time when the hinds calve?
Can you give the horse his strength? Do you clothe his neck with mane?
Is it by your wisdom that the hawk grows pinions, spreads his wings to the south?

Job answered God saying:

I knew that you can do everything, that nothing you propose is impossible to You. Who is this who obscures counsel without knowledge? Indeed I spoke without understanding of things beyond me which I did not know. Please listen and I will speak; I will ask you, and you will inform me. I had heard you with my ears, but now I see you with my eyes; therefore I will be distressed and I will be comforted on account of [my being] dust and ashes.

3. "God Everywhere"

Wheresoe'er I turn mine eyes
Around the earth or toward the skies
I see Thee in the starry field,
I see Thee in the harvest's yield,
In every breath, in every sound,
An echo of Thy name is found.
The blade of grass, the simple flower,
Bear witness to Thy matchless pow'r.
My every thought, Eternal God of heaven,
Ascends to Thee, to whom all praise be given.
—Rabbi Abraham Ibn Ezra, D.E. de L. translator, from *An Anthology of Medieval Hebrew Literature*.

4. Abraham was amazed by the vastness and the orderliness of the universe. Studying the sky, he thought at first that the sun must be the power that regulated it and directed everything. But evening came, and looking up at the sky, he saw that the sun had disappeared. Then he thought that perhaps it was the moon that was the directing force upon the world. But the very next morning, he observed that the moon was no more and that the sun had again taken its place. Thus contemplating the cosmos, he came to the conclusion that there must be a Power higher and above all those powers visible to the eyes of human beings, Who rules and orders the universe.
—Adapted from Genesis Rabbah 39:1 and Josephus, *Antiquities of the Jews*, ch.7.

5. Variety is the security of agriculture, as of biology. Unlike the "scientific" agriculturalists who give priority to "efficiency", the Andean farmers' first principle is variety. It is the ancient wisdom of putting the eggs into several baskets; in a season or a field in which one variety perishes, another, or several others, may thrive....One field, about the size of an ordinary living room, contained forty-six different potato varieties.
—Wendell Berry, *The Gift of Good Land,* p.8. Copyright © 1981 by Wendell Berry.

Purpose and Place

Text Study: Genesis 1:1-2:4

Participant Worksheet

Some people read the creation story as a literal or scientific account of how the world came into being. Many Jews, however, read this text as a story or origin myth whose primary purpose is to teach us about the nature of the Creator; about the plants, minerals and creatures that inhabit the earth and our relationship to them.

As you read this story, pay close attention to the themes that appear *repeatedly*.

1. How many times does the story say, "And God saw that this was good?" What does this tell us about the nature of creation? How does this apply to our "Useless Creatures" activity today?

2. Note the emphasis on the abundance of different kinds of species: vegetation and trees of every kind; living, creeping creatures of every kind, cattle; and every kind of wild beast. Why do you imagine God created so many species? Does the text place a value upon diversity? What ecological value does such diversity have?

3. On the third day, when God creates vegetation, the text emphasizes the seed-bearing capacity of each plant. Why?

4. *According to the text* do the various species belong to unique habitats, or can any one of them live anywhere?

5. Is there a reason for the particular order of the story? Is this a scientific or an evolutionary order? Is it a hierarchy of importance?

Purpose and Place

Text Study: Genesis 1:1-2:4

Leader Worksheet

Some people read the creation story as a literal or scientific account of how the world came into being. Many Jews, however, read this text as a story or origin myth whose primary purpose is to teach us about the nature of the Creator; about the plants, minerals and creatures that inhabit the earth and our relationship to them.

As you read this story, pay close attention to the key themes that appear in *repetition*.

1. How many times does the story say, "And God saw that this was good?" What does this tell us about the nature of creation? How does this apply to our "Useless Creatures" activity today?

"Good" occurs seven times. Umberto Cassuto, a modern Italian Bible scholar and literary critic, suggested that seven was a special number. The repetition of a word seven times identifies a particular word as the essence of a story. This is the case with the word brit *(covenant) in the Abraham and Isaac story (Genesis 22), where covenant is the theme. In this case "good" is the theme of the creation story. Everything that was created was good (has positive value, and is therefore not superfluous).*

It is interesting to compare our creation story with the creation story of other cultures. Many do not look upon created matter as good. The Gnostics, whose beliefs grew out of Platonic thought, held that only the soul is good, while the created material world is not good, and is the source of evil.

How do your perceptions about the world influence your treatment of it?

2. Note the emphasis on the abundance of different kinds of species: vegetation and trees of every kind, living, creeping creatures of every kind; cattle, and every kind of wild beast. Why do you imagine God created so many species? Does the text place a value upon diversity? What ecological value does such diversity have?

See the Wendell Berry text in the supplemental readings. Because of the great variety of creatures, creation has been able to continue despite major climatic changes and geological upheavals (and today, despite pesticides and other ecological deterrents). Only some species will be able to survive various changes and adapt to new habits. A wide range of diverse creatures insures that some will be pre-adapted to a new environment and will be able to survive. Diversity insures stability.

3. On the third day, when God creates vegetation, the text emphasizes the seed-bearing capacity of each plant. Why?

Through seeds, God has created a world that can perpetuate itself. Seeds are the blueprints for the continuation of creation. The seeds provide order to the creation process. Each species will continue to reproduce according to its kind, and according to its genetic makeup. Creation is neither random nor chaotic. The "seed-bearing" nature of the creation complements the "diverse" nature of creation. God has provided the possibility for change, growth and adaptation while maintaining underlying order and integrity.

4. According to the text do the various species belong to unique habitats, or can any one of them live anywhere?
Fish belong to water, birds belong to the air, humans and crawling things belong to the earth.

5. Is there a reason for the particular order of the story? Is this a scientific or an evolutionary order? Is it a hierarchy of importance?
In the first account of creation, Genesis 1, humans are created last. There are at least two understandings of this particular order.
1) Humans are the crowning glory of creation and may be considered the most important. A midrash (Jewish folklore) compares God's creation to a king's preparation for a banquet. The food is prepared, the table is set, all is made ready. Only then are the guests invited to come in to feast and rejoice. Similarly in this view of the creation story, the humans are created only after the rest of creation has been prepared for them.
2) Humans are created last, indicating they may be the least important. By creating them last, God is teaching humility. Remember, even the gnats were made before us!

1. Why does God dwell on the diversity of God's creation at such length?

2. What does the monologue about creation teach Job about God's justice?

3. After experiencing God's revelation of the diversity of God's creation, Job concludes that he is "dust and ashes." The text also implies that this conclusion—that he is dust and ashes—somehow comforts Job. What do you think was comforting about this for Job? From your perspective, would this thought bring you comfort at all? If yes, why? If no, why not?

4. Compare Job's experience with the times you have felt "small," humble or terrified when seeing God's presence in creation or in the vastness, diversity or power of nature. How have you felt in an earthquake, a tornado, a hurricane, a flood, visiting the Grand Canyon, hiking in the mountains, or canoeing in the wilderness?

Purpose and Place

Text Study: Selections from Job

Leader Worksheet

1. Why does God dwell on the diversity of God's creation at such length?
When you see the vastness and diversity of all of life, you see where you belong. God is giving Job an awesome tour of the universe to show him his place. If you only see yourself, your own small life and your own work, you may begin to think you know everything, have power over everything, or are in control of everything. You can lose sight of the richness of and magnificence of all of life. You forget the big picture. Job cannot judge things by his own standards; the human does not know all there is to know. Only God knows all there is to know .

2. What does the monologue about creation teach Job about God's justice?
Job can judge only by his own limited human standards. God is the ultimate judge, not humans.

3. After experiencing God's revelation of the diversity of God's creation, Job concludes that he is "dust and ashes." The text also implies that this conclusion—that he is dust and ashes—somehow comforts Job. What do you think was comforting about this for Job? From your perspective, would this thought bring you comfort at all? If yes, why? If no, why not?
Job finally knew his place and where he belonged, and knew that God was the ultimate owner of all life. For some of us, knowing our place can be an incredibly secure feeling. Remembering that God exists in everything can be comforting and uplifting. Some of us find comfort in earthquakes because they remind us of God's awesome power. Others may not be comforted by this at all!

4. Compare Job's experience with the times you have felt "small," humble or terrified when seeing God's presence in creation or in the vastness, diversity or power of nature. How have you felt in an earthquake, a tornado, a hurricane, a flood, visiting the Grand Canyon, hiking in the mountains, or canoeing in the wilderness?

Many environmentalists criticize the account of creation in Genesis, especially Genesis 1:28 in which God tells humanity to fill the earth and "master it". Their criticism lies in their conviction that as long as we see ourselves as masters or managers of the rest of the world, we will inevitably abuse our position and the earth. They go so far as to say that the Judeo-Christian tradition is responsible for the environmental crisis.

Some people say the earth doesn't need a manager. They say that the earth will heal only when humans relinquish all power and control and take their place alongside the rest of the natural world, rather than on top of it.

In this lesson we will consider the human's role in the story of creation, first by examining Genesis, and then by contemplating the writings of a few other thinkers. Given the widespread criticism of the biblical tradition, we will evaluate the terms of mastery that the story actually dictates. We will determine the obligations incumbent upon us as Jews and human beings.

OBJECTIVES

•Participants will understand how environmental problems have arisen as a result of human control and domination of nature.

•Participants will understand how Judaism views the position of humans in nature.

MATERIALS & PREPARATION

•Copies of the two articles in Readings & Worksheets (see Opening: Sample News Stories).

•Copies of Readings & Worksheets and Genesis 6 and 9.

•Ask participants to bring articles or personal stories about individuals who have helped the environment and their community.

•Copies of *Shomrei Adamah* Role Models

 OR

•Articles and pamphlets about organizations *in your area* whose projects involve environmental and human concerns. Check the Resource Section on environmental organizations at the back of this book.

The Human Place

Opening ▲

Use two accounts of the California dust storm (see Readings & Worksheets), or participants and leader may bring in two or more qualitatively different newspaper clippings of one event. Like the two dust storm articles, the different newspaper articles should supply the same basic facts but offer very different analyses of the issue.

Divide the group in half and give each sub-group copies (for each participant) of one of the clippings. One group will have Sample News Story 1 and the other, Sample News Story 2. *Do not reveal to the groups that they have received different articles.* Each group must summarize the information in its article. Reconvene and guide a discussion with the questions below.

DISCUSSION QUESTIONS

•Where did this event take place? Briefly summarize the facts of the event.

•What caused the accident?

•How many people were killed? How many injured?

•Could the DMV have prevented the accident?

•Why were the environmentalists blamed?

The two groups should provide similar answers for the above questions, but should begin to differ on the following issues. Allow the groups to argue their opinions.

- Who was really to blame for this dust storm?
- Is it natural for water to be scarce in this region?
- Can anything be done to prevent the dust storms in this region?

Now reveal the difference in the articles. Discuss the greater understanding readers obtain by reading several articles about an issue or event rather than reading just one. There are always multiple points of view to any issue, and multiple understandings of any situation. This may prove frustrating at times, but it is the nature of diversity and difference.

We can learn from and work with the tension of differences. In trying to resolve differences, we are forced to know ourselves and substantiate our position when we would otherwise become lazy. Ultimately, the resolution of differences gives us an expanded view of life by allowing us come to grips with opposing world views.

The *Torah* sometimes contains two separate accounts of the same story. To understand the intention of the author, it is critical to take both stories into account. A single account of any story provides only a limited view. You may want to include, as an example, Deuteronomy 19:21, the passage that instructs us to reciprocate our enemy's blows, "an eye for an eye, a tooth for a tooth. . ." Taken out of context, or without further examination of later Jewish texts, this passage can be gravely misused.

Text Study: The Creation Story ▲▲

The story of the creation of humans is told two times in the Bible. Pair participants off and have them read aloud to each other excerpts of the two versions: Genesis 1:24-28 and Genesis 2:4-9, 15. It is important here to pay attention to the way in which the two stories are told; pay careful attention to the words that are used and the mood that is created. You will find discussion questions in the Readings & Worksheets section of this chapter. Pairs should use these questions as guidelines in formulating their own opinions of the texts. After ten minutes, regroup and use the questions provided to guide a discussion of the place of humans in creation.

Getting Involved: *Shomrei Adamah* Role Models ▲▲

Divide the group into sub-groups of 4 or 5. Using the articles and stories participants have brought in, or the ones at the back of the chapter, give each group two or three articles to discuss (groups can have the same or different articles), along with any personal stories they may have. While groups are at work, you may want to offer some of the following questions as guidelines, perhaps by writing them on the board.

34

DISCUSSION QUESTIONS

•How do these projects relate to the environment?

•How do they help our human communities?

•What do you think motivates people to do these things?

•How do you think these individuals feel after doing these things?

Group members should consider one small personal environmentally helpful act they will do within the week. Individuals should make commitments to their groups to follow through with their acts. Set up a calendar to chart follow-ups.

OR

Divide participants into 3 or 4 groups. Have each group explore the resources (see Resource Section at end of book), and choose an organization they would like to know more about. Each group will need to pick a spokesperson to call the organization and set up a time when the group can meet with a representative, go to the headquarters for an orientation, or visit a project with a guide. They will need to complete this before beginning the unit on "Ecology, Judaism and *Tikkun Olam*." See that unit for a follow-up activity.

Text Study: The Covenantal Relationship ▲▲▲

We can better understand the Jewish approach to nature by examining a central theme in Jewish thought, the covenant. A covenant is a special contract between two parties. It usually involves a commitment between God and human beings. In the covenant, God makes some promises and the other party accepts some obligations. Unlike a contract, in a covenantal relationship, a loving, long-term, responsible relationship is implied.

Monford Harris, a contemporary Jewish philosopher, believes that the covenant between God and humans is the model for all human relationships: between human and God, between human and human, and between human and nature. Harris believes that this model of relationship is one way to define us as Jews. It is different from the Greek model, which focused on a person's mind and spirit. Hellenic people valued human self-sufficiency above human connections and relationships.

•What, then, are the implications of a covenantal relationship vis-à-vis the human relationship with nature?
Because the covenental relationship is part of the Jewish worldview it would be incongruous for a Jew to exploit others or nature. Relationship means that there are two parties in a mutual act of relating. If humans were to control nature this would not be mutualism but rather, exploitation. One being may be more poweful than the other in a relationship but the presupposition is that neither will abuse their position. This understanding of relationship and covenant stems from the assumption that everything on earth is inherently valuable.

35

•Divide everyone into 3 groups for text study. Each group will receive one of the three readings (see Readings & Worksheets for Genesis chapters 6 and 9, Martin Buber, and Wendell Berry). They will also receive the discussion questions that accompany their text. As they begin to read, have them think about the following questions:

•What is the covenantal relationship, and what does it mean with regard to our position in nature? How does this relationship ultimately define our actions?

•In ten minutes everyone should regroup; a spokesperson from each group can summarize that group's text and discuss its significance for the covenantal relationship. The leader can keep participants on track by addressing some of the discussion questions provided on the worksheets.

Bringing It Home ▲

To conclude, have a volunteer read the following passage. Participants should think about their own relationships with the world around them. How do they define their place in the world, and their responsibility to that place? We will examine this concept more closely in a unit on the "Web of Life."

Two men were sailing on a boat when one of them began taking animal skins out of his bag to let them dry. The skins stank and the second man asked the first to put the skins away. The first answered, "What I do at my own seat is not your business." The second man thought for a moment and them took out a carpenter's drill. He began drilling a hole under his seat. The first man jumped up and said, "Are you crazy? You're going to kill us." The second man replied, "What I do at my own seat is not your business."
—Adapted from Leviticus Rabbah 4:6.

For Further Reading

Wendell Berry, *Home Economics*

Wendell Berry, *Continuous Harmony*

Wendell Berry, *The Gift of Good Land*

Roderick Frazier Nash, *The Rights of Nature: A History of Environmental Ethics*

Thedore Goldfarb, *Taking Sides: Clashing Views on Controversial Environmental Issues*

Thomas Berry, *The Dream of the Earth*

Aldo Leopold, *A Sand County Alamanac*

BLINDING DUST STORM DEADLY

Fresno, CA—Cold, hard wind blew drought-dry Central Valley earth into a deadly dust storm Friday, setting up traffic pileups that killed at least 14 Thanksgiving holiday travelers and injured 150 along Interstate 5 south of Los Banos.

The latest in a series of drought-caused dust storms created a chain-reaction disaster that sent helicopters, ambulances and hospitals into action. All available emergency crews from surrounding towns responded to a scene of crashed vehicles and broken bodies covered with dust and blood.

Winds were estimated at 45 miles per hour.

Along I-5, smashed cars and trucks acted as all but invisible roadblocks to oncoming traffic. Travelers on their Thanksgiving holiday could not stop in time to keep their vehicles from smashing into others already stalled. Screaming and moaning accident victims looked for help in clouds of dust.

One driver said he was headed home for the holiday when his car was suddenly surrounded by a dust storm.

"Visibility came and went and this time it went all of a sudden," he said.

A Central Valley farmer blamed the drought on environmentalist groups, saying that if all the proposed dams had been approved, there would be no drought. Much irrigation water is required for farming in this semi-arid region. State officials have come under criticism for not providing more irrigation water to the farmers when they adjusted allotments because of drought.

The Department of Motor Vehicles (DMV) had information about dust flurries in the area hours before the accident occurred. Many criticized the DMV for not closing the highway before such a disaster could happen. Sections of I-5 are often closed in the Central Valley in the winter dowing to the Tule fog.

The DMV is reviewing its warning procedure to avoid future disasters. Officials say there are plans for a new early-warning system.

DEADLY DUST STORM

Fresno, CA—Cold, hard wind blew drought-dry Central Valley earth into a deadly dust storm Friday, setting up traffic pileups that killed at least 14 Thanksgiving holiday travelers and injured 150 along Interstate 5 south of Los Banos.

The latest in a series of drought-caused dust storms created a chain-reaction disaster that sent helicopters, ambulances and hospitals into action. All available emergency crews from surrounding towns responded to a scene of crashed vehicles and broken bodies covered with dust and blood.

Winds were estimated at 45 miles per hour.

Along I-5, smashed cars and trucks acted as all but invisible roadblocks to oncoming traffic. Travelers on their Thanksgiving holiday could not stop in time to keep their vehicles from smashing into others already stalled. Screaming and moaning accident victims looked for help in clouds of dust.

One driver said he was headed home for the holiday when his car was suddenly surrounded by a dust storm.

"Visibility came and went and this time it went all of a sudden," he said.

Recriminations followed the terrible pileup, aimed at the Department of Motor Vehicles (DMV), environmentalists, and the drought. In 1981 the President's Commission on Environmental Quality described the South Valley as "one of the few areas that has suffered from all the major forces of desertification." This was after the commission studied a 1977 Valley dust storm that blew up 25 million tons of topsoil. In fact, dust is not the area's true disease, but rather a mere symptom. Few people know that this region once contained the largest body of fresh water in the western United States, Tulare Lake. But the supplying rivers were diverted for irrigation, and most of the wetland drained for agriculture.

Many journalists have blamed the drought for this tragic accident, but the valley's whole history of human intervention is the real culprit. At the time of the accident, if you had stood in the area and turned 360 degrees, all you would have seen for miles in any direction would have been plowed soil. There is no organic matter left in the soil, and no ground cover, both of which would keep the soil moist, preventing the winds from lifting it into the air.

Will an early-warning system proposed by the DMV prevent a repetition of this disaster in the future? It may prevent accidents, but it cannot prevent the dust storms.

The Human Place

Text Study: The Creation Story

Participant Worksheet

1. What is Adam to "do" in the first story?

2. What is Adam to do in the second story?

3. How is the human created in the first story? And in the second? Does this help you understand the different ways the creation and role of human beings is understood in the two accounts?

4. What is the mood or tone of each story? Of what other types of stories do the two accounts remind you? What about each story's pace? Does this give you any more clues about Adam in each account?

5. Are these two perspectives and stories contradictory, or are they complementary? Do the stories offer us a model of human behavior toward the earth and the species? Are we to reflect one or the other or both? Can a person integrate both of these perspectives? How?

6. What might the Bible be telling us by presenting two different accounts?

7. What would the world be like if humans totally reflected the Adam of the first story? Of the second story? Which story does our world reflect today? Remember to recognize both the good and bad sides of each story.

8. Some people say the earth doesn't need a manager. They say that the earth will heal only when humans relinquish all power and control and take their place alongside the rest of the natural world, rather than on top of it. According to each of these creation tales, should humans "manage" the earth? What do you think it will take to heal the earth, according to these stories and in you own opinion?

9. Besides what you have already learned about the two stories, can you imagine any other interpretations of Genesis 1:28? Do you feel that humans have a unique role on earth—or is our place in the web of life no more (or less) important than that of any other creature?

10. How do you understand God's command to till and tend our gardens on a metaphorical level? What does it mean to you to act as keepers of the earth? Why do you think the national Jewish environmental resource center chose the name "*Shomrei Adamah*"—"Keepers of the Earth"?

The Human Place

Text Study: The Creation Story

Leader Worksheet

1. What is Adam to "do" in the first story?
To have dominion over the fish of the sea, the fowl of the air, the cattle, and all the earth.
To fill the earth and replenish it and to "master" the earth.

2. What is Adam to do in the second story?
To serve and to keep the garden (If you read Hebrew, pay attention to the verbs here, la'avod (to work) and leeshmor (to guard). Think about other biblical contexts in which these verbs are used.

3. How is the human created in the first story? In the second? Does this help you understand the different ways the creation and role of human beings is understood in the two accounts?
a. In the first account, God formed humans on the sixth day, creating male and female in God's own image. In this story, humans are formed in the image of an omnipotent, ever-present, all-powerful ruler, and are given a role that imitates the domineering qualities of their maker.
b. In the second account, God formed man of the dust of the ground and breathed into his nostrils the breath of life. Thus man became a living soul. In this account, human is created from the earth, in working and guarding the earth, he is also serving God.

4. What is the mood or tone of each story? Of what other types of stories do the two accounts remind you? What about each story's pace? Does this give you any more clues about Adam in each acount?
a. In the first story, there is a linear progression that is very orderly, organized and highly controlled; on each day a particular variety of creature is created to fit into a prescribed plan. You get the feeling that everything is perfectly orchestrated from above. God is creating a place for everything. Some people may get a sense that this story of creation resembles a perfectly running machine.
b. In the second story, you get a sense that someone is telling you a story. Out of the mist that watered the earth; in other words, out of mud, God made man. God formed Adam out of clay and then blew into him to give him life. Notice the words adam (earthling) and adamah(earth) are used here; the absolute link between Adam—and all subsequent earthlings—and the earth must be taken very seriously.

5. Are these two perspectives and stories contradictory, or are they complementary? Do the stories offer us a model of human behavior toward the earth and the species? Are we to reflect one or the other or both? Can a person integrate both of these perspectives? How?
The perspectives are complementary; sometimes we use our mastery to build, create, and learn as God and Adam do in the first creation story. Other times, we experience

40

a different sense of time and place. We may find ourselves more receptive and open to all of life; we go beyond our daily mundane tasks and beyond our usual belief that we are in control of our lives. We may have an experience of awe or wonder, moved by a power greater than ourselves, or we may find ourselves wanting to serve God by guarding and working the earth.

6. What might the Bible be telling us by presenting two different accounts?
Neither version's world view or behavior stands alone. Together they reflect the underlying tension of the human condition, human nature. However, these conflicting views present a unique challenge to the human species. Human beings must balance the behavior of dominating or controlling the earth and appreciating, respecting, serving and keeping the earth. This is no easy task.

7. What would the world be like if humans totally reflected the Adam of the first story? Of the second story? Which story does our world reflect today? Remember to recognize both the good and bad sides of each story.

8. Some people say the earth doesn't need a manager. They say that the earth will heal only when humans relinquish all power and control and take their place alongside the rest of the natural world, rather than on top of it. According to each of these creation tales, should humans "manage" the earth? What do you think it will take to heal the earth, according to these stories and in your own opinion?
At this point in the class discussion, refer participants to the environmental trend in attacking Genesis and the Judeo-Christian tradition described in this unit's introduction. Use the question above to encourage them to take a stand on this real-life debate.

9. Besides what you have already learned about the two stories, can you imagine any other interpretations of Genesis 1:28? Do you feel that humans have a unique role on earth—or is our place in the web of life no more (or less) important than that of any other creature?
One fact remains: Whether we like it or not, we are the only species that has the power to either preserve or destroy the entire web of life.

10. How do you understand God's command to till and tend our gardens on a metaphorical level? What does it mean to you to act as keepers of the earth? Why do you think the national Jewish environmental resource center chose the name "*Shomrei Adamah*"—"Keepers of the Earth"?

The Human Place

Text Study: The Covenantal Relationship: #1: Genesis 6:17-21 and 9:8-11

Participant Worksheet

A closer reading of this well-known tale reveals several lessons about humanity, the creation and our role in the world. As you read the sections from the Noah story, consider these questions: With whom does God make a covenant? What obligations does this covenant entail?

1. Why does God decide to destroy the world?

2. The text provides an answer to question #1, but this is a very general statement. What exactly is the world's evil? And, more vexing, are the animals and plants to blame? Why do they suffer—are they capable of evil?

3. Why does God ask Noah to take a pair of every kind of living creature into the ark?

4. After the flood ends, God establishes a covenant (symbolized by the rainbow). This covenant is not just with Noah and his family, but rather with every living creature that came out of the ark. What does God promise to do in this covenant?

5. Why does God make this covenant with *all* creation?

6. What obligations and privileges does this covenant create for humankind? For other creatures?

The Human Place

Text Study: The Covenantal Relationship: #1: Genesis 6:17-21 and 9:8-11

Leader Worksheet

A closer reading of this well-known tale reveals several lessons about humanity, the creation and our role in the world. As you read the sections from the Noah story, consider these questions: With whom does God make a covenant? What obligations does this covenant entail?

1. Why does God decide to destroy the world?
It is evil, corrupt and filled with lawlessness (see Genesis 6:11-14).

2. The text provides an answer to question #1, but this is a very general statement. What exactly is the world's evil? And, more vexing, are the animals and plants to blame? Why do they suffer—are they capable of evil?
Animals and plants are not to blame. Only humans make moral choices, yet the rest of creation often suffers as a consequence of the decisions we make. Plants and other animals suffer because they bear the consequences of human action and inaction, not because they are being punished.

3. Why does God ask Noah to take a pair of every kind of living creature into the ark?
Emphasize the importance of diversity. Every single species is important to God, and therefore worthy of living. As the Midrash *in Genesis Rabbah teaches (see previous chapter), no creature in the world is superfluous; each has a role.*

4. After the flood ends, God establishes a covenant (symbolized by the rainbow). This covenant is not just with Noah and his family, but rather with every living creature that came out of the ark. What does God promise to do in this covenant?
To never again destroy the earth.

5. Why does God make this covenant with *all* creation?
Perhaps because every aspect of creation is of vital importance—again, emphasizing the value of diversity.

6. What obligations and privileges does this covenant create for humankind? For other creatures?
Traditionally, our rabbis saw this covenant as the Scriptural basis for establishing the seven most basic moral laws that are binding on all humanity, not just Jews. These are called the Noahide laws and they are: prohibitions against idolatry, blasphemy, bloodshed, sexual immorality, theft, cruelty to animals and the injunction to establish a legal system.
We are all privileged to reproduce and fill the earth with our offspring and to thrive therein.

Text Study: The Covenantal Relationship: #2: from Martin Buber, I *and Thou*, p. 57

Reading

I can contemplate a tree.

I can accept it as a picture: a rigid pillar in a flood of light, or splashes of green traversed by the gentleness of the blue silver ground.

I can feel it as a movement: the flowing veins around the sturdy, striving core, the sucking of the roots, the breathing of the leaves, the infinite commerce with earth and air, and the growing itself in its darkness.

I can assign it to a species and observe it as an instance, with an eye to its construction and its way of life.

I can overcome its uniqueness and form so rigorously that I recognize it only as an expression of the law; those laws according to which the elements mix and separate.

I can dissolve it into a number, into a pure relation between numbers, and eternalize it.

Throughout all of this the tree remains my object and has its place and its time span, its kind and condition.

But it can also happen, if will and grace are joined, that as I contemplate the tree I am drawn into a relation, and the tree ceases to be an It. The power of exclusiveness has seized me.

This does not require me to forgo any of the modes of contemplation. There is nothing that I must not see in order to see, and there is no knowledge that I must forget. Rather is everything, picture and movement, species and instance, law and number included and inseparably fused.

Whatever belongs to the tree is included: its form and its mechanics, its colors and its chemistry, its conversation with the elements and its conversation with the stars; all this in its entirety.

1. We spoke about perception in the "Seeing" unit. How does Buber expand on what we know about paying attention to detail?

2. What are the different ways we can look at a tree?

3. In your opinion, what kind of person would see the tree from each of the different viewpoints? For instance, would a person who views trees as "an expression of the law" come from a particular religious or philosophical background, or have a particular career?

4. How do you usually view a tree? In your view, what is the proper treatment of the tree?

5. Given Buber's understanding of the tree, how should you act toward trees?

The Human Place

Text Study: The Covenantal Relationship: #2: from Martin Buber

Leader Worksheet

1. We spoke about perception in the "Seeing" unit. How does Buber expand on what we know about paying attention to detail?

He teaches us that there is a multitude of points of view of the tree; each point of view will reveal the tree in a different way.

2. What are the different ways we can look at a tree?
   a. as a picture
   b. as a feeling, a life process
   c. as a species with a particular way of life
   d. as a mixture of elements
   e. as a number or an abstraction
   f. we can be one with the tree

3. In your opinion, what kind of person would see the tree from each of the different viewpoints? For instance, would a person who views trees as "an expression of the law" come from a particular religious or philosophical background, or have a particular career?

Some possibilities:
   a. an artist or a layperson
   b. a humanist or poet
   c. a biologist
   d. a chemist
   e. a mathematician
   f. a religious person, a transcendentalist

4. How do you usually view a tree? In your view, what is the proper treatment of the tree?

5. Given Buber's understanding of the tree, how should you act toward trees?

Text Study: The Covenantal Relationship: #3: from Wendell Berry, *A Continuous Harmony*, pp.159-162

Reading

The Likenesses of Atonement

Living in our speech, though no longer in our consciousness, is an ancient system of analogies that clarifies a series of mutually defining and sustaining unities: of farmer and field, of husband and wife, of the world and God. The language of both of our literature and of our everyday speech is full of references and allusions to this expansive metaphor of farming and marriage and worship. A man planting crops is like a man making love to his wife and vice versa: he is a husband or a husbandman. A man praying is like a lover, or he is like a plant in a field waiting for rain. As husbandman, a man is both the steward and the likeness of God, the greatest husbandman. God is the lover of the world and its faithful husband.

All the essential relationships are comprehended in this metaphor. A farmer's relation to his land is the basic and central connection in the relation of humanity to the creation; the agricultural relation stands for the larger relation. Similarly, marriage is the basic and central community tie; it begins and stands for the relation we have to family and to the larger circles of human association. And these relationships to the creation and to the human community are in turn basic to, and may stand for, our relationship to God—or to the sustaining mysteries and powers of the creation.

Thus if the metaphor of atonement is alive in his consciousness, he will see that he should love and care for his land as for his wife, that his relation to his place in the world is as solemn and demanding and as blessed as marriage; and he will see that he should respect his marriage as he respects the mysteries and transcendent powers —that is as a sacrament. Or—to move in the opposite direction through the changes of the metaphor—in order to care properly for his land he will see that he must emulate the Creator: to learn to use and preserve the open fields, as Sir Albert Howard said, he must look into the woods; he must study and follow the natural process; he must understand the husbanding that, in nature, always accompanies providing.

Like any interlinking system, this one fails in the failure of any one of its parts. When we obscure or corrupt our understanding of any one of the basic unities, we begin to misunderstand all of them. The vital knowledge dies out of our consciousness and becomes fossilized in our speech and culture. This is our condition now. We have severed the vital links of the atonement metaphor, and we did this initially, I think, by degrading and obscuring our connection to the land, by looking upon the land as merchandise and ourselves as its traveling salesmen.

The Human Place

Text Study: The Covenantal Relationship: #3: from Wendell Berry

Participant Worksheet

1) Berry employs a series of metaphors to describe the relationship betwen humanity and the land by linking farming with marriage and worship. Can you think of any analogies from Jewish tradition?

2) Compare Berry's linkage of stewardship, marriage and worship with the Jewish notion of covenant. Note that our tradition often uses the language of marriage to describe God's covenant with humanity (for numerous examples see the Book of Hosea). What, according to Jewish tradition, would be our obligations as partners in the covenant?

3) Berry states that "A farmer's relation to his land is the basic and central connection in the relation of humanity to the creation; the agricultural relation stands for the larger relation. Similarly, marriage is the basic and central community tie...." Most Americans today are not farmers, and furthermore, many of us would point to analogies other than marriage as a just and praiseworthy paradigm of human relations. What metaphors of relationships might we propose which take into account the realities of contemporary American Jewish life and at the same time accurately reflect our covenental bond with the earth?

4) Berry's many references to "man" and husbandry are in keeping with the use of these terms when he wrote this work in 1973. How might the passage read differently if approached from a feminist perspective? Do you think women approach relationships with other people and the planet in a way that is essentially different from their male counterparts?

The Human Place

Text Study: The Covenantal Relationship: #3: from Wendell Berry

Leader Worksheet

1) Berry employs a series of metaphors to describe the relationship betwen humanity and the land by linking farming with marriage and worship. Can you think of any analogies from Jewish tradition?

For example, the word for work (including working the land) and the word for worship are the same — avodah. Both prayer and productive stewardship are obligations in our tradition.

2) Compare Berry's linkage of stewardship, marriage and worship with the Jewish notion of covenant. Note that our tradition often uses the language of marriage to describe God's covenant with humanity (for numerous examples see the Book of Hosea). What, according to Jewish tradition, would be our obligations as partners in the covenant?

Respect and support.

3) Berry states that "A farmer's relation to his land is the basic and central connection in the relation of humanity to the creation; the agricultural relation stands for the larger relation. Similarly, marriage is the basic and central community tie...." Most Americans today are not farmers, and furthermore, many of us would point to analogies other than marriage as a just and praiseworthy paradigm of human relations. What metaphors of relationships might we propose which take into account the realities of contemporary American Jewish life and at the same time accurately reflect our covenental bond with the earth?

Parent-child, friendship, siblings.

4) Berry's many references to "man" and husbandry are in keeping with the use of these terms when he wrote this work in 1973. How might the passage read differently if approached from a feminist perspective? Do you think women approach relationships with other people and the planet in a way that is essentially different from their male counterparts?

The Human Place

Shomrei Adamah Role Models

Reading

BECOMING TREEPEOPLE

by Katie & Andy Lipkis

We have the chance ... to be the first to live in final accord with our Spaceship Earth – and
hence in final harmony with each other. The Ancient Greeks, the Renaissance communities, the
founders of America, the Victorians enjoyed no
such challenge as this. What a time to be alive!
– *Norman Myers, 1984*

The publicity surrounding our organization [TreePeople in Los Angeles] is often focused on our "heroic" work. Although the attention is flattering, it misses the point. This work is wonderful and miraculous, but it is available to everyone. This is profoundly local and personal work, and everyone who embarks on this journey is a hero – or none of us are.

Our work feeds us. Planting and caring for trees, taking on challenges bigger than ourselves, building bridges of cooperation, solving problems creatively, seeing communities grow and get stronger, watching people come into their power, having a purpose, knowing that we have made a difference in the lives of others – all this produces a satisfaction so deep and fulfilling we feel like millionaires. In a sense we are. Instead of dollars earned, millions of trees are planted and nurtured, lives are touched, kids are turned on and caring.

The clutter of modern life interferes with our ability to see.

ANDY:

I started the work that became TreePeople in 1970 when I was fifteen years old. Although the vehicle was trees, my motivation was the search for a life of meaning in a world that appeared self-serving.

In high school, I was starting to feel my power, while the world was broadcasting the message that I couldn't really do anything to affect anything. It was frustrating and painful.

In the midst of this, I learned that the forest where I spent my summers was being killed by the drifting smog from Los Angeles. I spent three weeks with two dozen summer camp peers, working like crazy to repair a piece of the dying forest by planting smog-tolerant trees. Instead of sitting around figuring out what to do for entertainment, we swung picks at rock-hard ground and shoveled cow manure. When it was done, we watched birds, squirrels, grass, flowers and trees return to what had been a dead parking lot. Caring friendships developed while we were having what amounted to one of the highest times of our lives.

The experience filled me with ideas for repairing what I saw as an environmentally and socially damaged world.

What followed was three years of repeatedly trying – and failing – before my project started to take shape. There were many barriers to confront. People who cared about the environment were portrayed on television as weird outcasts, and people who expressed concern were do-gooders. I didn't want to look like a freak. Although I was drawn to the work, I resisted it. If it *worked*, would I get stuck doing this for life?

KATIE:

I was definitely not a do-gooder. In fact, I was a pretty average sort of ignorant person who rode a motorcycle and jumped out of airplanes.

When I met Andy, I'd never even planted a tree. I'd had a lot of fun working my way up the advertising ladder, grabbing a Clio award on the way, and had reached the rung called "Is that all there is?" But the trappings of corporate power literally had me trapped. How could I survive without a huge salary? What could I do to earn money? Copywriting was so easy! Ironically, I felt powerless. There was so much on Earth to be done, and my 9-5 felt like marking time. I was happiest volunteering, giving something back, using my powers of persuasion for things that could make the world a better place and relieve suffering. I wanted to find a way to share and nurture the blossoming of real power in others.

In a moment of rare objectivity, while standing in my air-conditioned office next to my ficus that I didn't even know was a ficus, I was able to say, "When you've given this up, and the money starts looking attractive, remember this instant; the money's not worth it!"

A conference came to Melbourne, Australia, where I was living, and one of the speakers was a young man whose dream was to see a million trees planted in Los Angeles. "What do you do?" he asked. "I write," I replied. "Boy oh boy, could TreePeople use a writer!" he exclaimed. We were married and are living happily ever after....

From their upcoming book, The Simple Act of Planting a Tree, *J.P. Tarcher publishers. Contact Katie and Andy Lipkis (and TreePeople) at 12601 Mulholland Dr., Beverly Hills, CA 90210.*

Reprinted from *IN CONTEXT* / No. 26, pp. 45-46.

A Friend of Canada's Forests Battles Loggers

TO many observers, Canada's rich carpet of forests looks vast enough to withstand any amount of logging.

Not to Colleen McCrory. A native of British Columbia, the province that supplies half of Canada's annual timber harvest, she scarcely notices the forests around her for all the missing trees.

This winner of a 1992 Goldman Environmental Prize, who is a single mother of three, says that both her province and her nation are at a crisis point that stems from overlogging and poor forest management.

Canada's rapid rate of deforestation, she says, is now very similar to that of Brazil. Just in British Columbia, she says, some 600,000 acres of trees are felled each year, more than the annual yield from all US national forests.

At considerable personal risk, Ms. McCrory has spent most of the last two decades trying to get more wilderness areas set aside in British Columbia. She urges Canadians everywhere to be alert to the dangers of overcutting their top export.

"I worked on that little dot for eight years," she says, pointing to a small green area on a map of British Columbia during a recent in-

MCCRORY: *The environmental activist is a single mother of three.*

terview here. She says the Valhalla Society, which she helped to found in 1975 and currently chairs, finally persuaded government officials in 1983 to establish Valhalla Provincial Park, the green "dot" on her map. She went on to co-found the National Save South Moresby Committee, which in 1987 convinced authorities to establish a national marine reserve and park 1,000 miles to the west in the Queen Charlotte Islands. McCrory says the two parks add up to "little shining glimmers of hope for what really needs to be done."

"We have some of the last and most spectacular wilderness areas left in the world ... but we're losing on so many fronts," McCrory explains. "Industry is pushing logging roads into areas we've identified as needing protection. I think our key success so far is in raising public awareness."

She grew up eating deer meat and macaroni as one in a family of nine children in the small village of New Denver in the heavily forested Valhalla Valley. Her environmental concern blossomed in the 1970s when she noticed that vast stretches of side valleys were being clearcut by loggers. "We realized it was only a matter of time before they came to the main valley," she says, recalling the start of the Valhalla Society.

The logging industry reacted strongly to the criticism against them with what she terms a "smear" campaign. Loggers said she and others were extremists bent on destroying jobs. Her children were harrassed. Eventually she was forced to liquidate the small clothing business she owned.

"People quit shopping in my store," she says. "It was a well-organized hate campaign that's been going on for years."

McCrory insists she is not against logging. Indeed, she argues that if forests are felled at the current pace and under present conditions, loggers will work themselves out of a job. "It's a matter of having respect for the forests so you don't destroy the whole ecosystem," she explains.

McCrory also argues that more efficient management of the forests, including further processing of timber within Canada before export, could also do much to save jobs.

Still, in her view, better management is no substitute for the need to preserve more areas of natural beauty as living museums.

"They're taking down too much," she says of the loggers. "We need a balance that allows parts of the ecosystem not to be logged at all."

McCrory's forest interests are increasingly national these days. In the last two years, she has campaigned vigorously against an influx of large new pulp mills across northern Canada.

Recently she helped form an umbrella group of concerned Canadians called the Future Forest Alliance. Her dream, she says, is to preserve 12 percent of Canada's land base as wilderness.

– Lucia Mouat

Reprinted from *The Christian Science Monitor,* May 12, 1992, p. 14

FREE TOILETS

Never say the best things in life aren't free. Henry "Hank" Ryan, a resident of Winsted, Connecticut, offered 50 special water-saving toilets to his neighbors around Highland Lake last summer for a price he hoped they couldn't refuse: free. Ryan said he was concerned about sewage wastes leaching into the lake from substandard septic systems. A friend donated the Venezuelan-manufactured toilets which use only 1.5 gallons per flush rather than the profligate 7 gallons used in toilets most Americans have. Installation was included in the deal.

Ryan was swamped with calls, receiving 22 requests in one day. He installed a total of 35 toilets on the weekends, decreasing water use around the lake by 60 percent. The first toilet was delivered bearing a bouquet of flowers in its portal. "Humor is one way to break apathy," advises Ryan. "The issue of the environment is a train coming down the tracks. By putting some humor in it, people are willing to listen."

Conservation hasn't come new to Ryan, who is the proprietor of Winsted's only Mexican food restaurant, the Cafe de Ola, when he is not passing out toilets. He has been promoting tree planting programs along Winsted's Main Street for the past ten years. "Conservation is empowerment," Ryan says, admitting a crisis-oriented personality which impassions his interest in conservation. "What it does is to give people the opportunity to get out from under economic oppression, which eventually becomes political oppression."

For more information, contact First Conserve, 11 Willow St., Winsted, CT 06098, (203) 379-9132.

Reprinted from *Buzzman,* Volume II, No. 1, January/February 1990

Mining Recyclables from Our Garbage

PROFILE

Where most people see garbage, Dan Knapp sees valuable resources. A Berkeley, California, resident with a lumberjack's build, Dan co-founded a profitable company based on the premise that we can recycle almost all of what we now dismiss as "garbage." His company, called Urban Ore, grossed over $600,000 in 1989 by selling goods rescued from the trash bin.

Urban Ore's sales yard, occupying a paved lot just a few hundred yards from Berkeley's garbage transfer station, looks like a giant garage sale. Rows of furniture line one end of the lot: a sectional sofa with matching barstools, a mahogany sideboard, dressers, kitchen chairs — just about anything you'd need to furnish your apartment. Stacks of crates are crammed with sundry items: a muffin tin, hangers, a bottle of cologne, a tool kit, even a surfboard. Less than 25 percent comes from workers sorting through city waste; the rest is dropped off by residents. "It's cheaper than paying the tipping fee at the transfer station," Dan explains.

Dan believes the residential and commercial discards he sells would all be landfilled if Urban Ore didn't exist. The company is an exemplary part of his crusade to convince people that "total recycling" is not only possible, but also profitable. He points to the wealth of potentially recyclable materials often trashed: metals like brass and copper that would command a high price if sorted by grade; concrete that could be ground into gravel for landscaping or pavement; lumber that could be cleaned and resold; and the kind of reusable merchandise he sells at Urban Ore. He and his wife Mary Lou Deventer have contracted with University of California Press to write a book that will describe ways to recycle almost everything we throw away.

Dan's entry into the world of trash wasn't typical of most salvage-yard operators. He holds a Ph.D. in sociology and was once a university professor. He undertook his journey from the groves of academe to the hills of landfilled refuse after he discovered the economic potential buried in garbage while hauling trash for a food co-op in Eugene, Oregon.

He volunteered for the weekly trek to the dump because he owned the perfect vehicle for the job — a 1948 GMC flatbed named "Fred Jackson." There, he discovered a treasure trove of valuable materials like hardware and lumber. He began challenging himself to return from the landfill with as much material as he discarded, ignoring the signs warning that salvaging was illegal.

One day, Dan eyed a dump operator frowning at him from across mountains of trash as he loaded discarded lumber onto Fred Jackson. Moments later, the man was charging him with a bulldozer — blade down. Dan leaped into Fred Jackson and slammed the door just as the bulldozer mauled the pile of lumber he had been collecting. The near miss left him shaken: "I couldn't believe that somebody was willing to kill to enforce a policy of needless destruction," he says.

After the bulldozer incident, Dan told himself: "Don't get mad, get even." He landed a job as head of the county office that was exploring ways to solve the Eugene area's garbage glut.

Lane County (where Eugene is located) had just purchased a $3.5 million refuse-derived fuel plant that was supposed to convert garbage to fuel for industrial boilers. After three months of study, he concluded that the plant would produce inferior fuel for a nearly nonexistent market, and that sparks from its garbage shredder could ignite flammable materials in the waste. He recommended that Lane County reduce its wastestream with labor-intensive recycling — like composting yard waste and pre-sorting metals. Convinced that the refuse-derived fuel plant would work, the commissioners fired Dan by cutting his funding. (Incidentally, the plant exploded in 1980, when a spark from the shredder ignited toluene vapor from wood filler in a piece of plywood, according to Mike Turner of the Lane County Solid Waste Division, who was there at the time.)

Out of money and out of patience, Dan hitchhiked from Eugene to Berkeley with only a backpack and $40. Three days later, he was working at the Berkeley dump, salvaging metal for $4 per hour. At the time, he viewed himself as a "participant observer" — a sociologist who studies by doing. The dump environment — the haulers, operators, and waste — became his area of expertise.

In 1980, Dan and two garbage colleagues rented a lot near the San Francisco Bay waterfront for $500 per month. They began selling building materials retrieved from the Berkleley dump. Profits from the sale of salvaged scrap metal paid the first month's rent — hence the name "Urban Ore."

The company has grown rapidly from its humble origins. It now employs 16 workers at two salvage yards. The first lot, the Building Materials Exchange, sells salvaged doors, windows, bathtubs, and sinks to renovators, restorers, artists, and landlords. The other yard, called the Discard Management Center, offers everything from furniture to clothing to kitchen appliances. Customers range from "pack rats" (as one Urban Ore employee describes them) to antique dealers.

Dan's current job description is a world apart from his early work in the salvage business, when he burrowed into landfills amidst ample rat populations and dive-bombing seagulls. These days, he spends most of his time confronting the type of office work that plagues every entrepreneur: spreadsheets and payrolls, lawyers and insurance agents. He jets across the country to expound on the untapped possibilities of recycling. At a recycling conference in Los Angeles one weekend, and a legislative conference in Chicago two weeks later, Dan Knapp preached his primary motto: "Waste isn't waste until it's wasted."

— *Jackie MacDonald*

Reprinted from *Garbage*, September/October 1990

Citizen Baykeeper

PROFILE

The 26-foot skiff *Baykeeper* plows through the choppy, ebony waters of the Arthur Kill, a polluted tidal strait splitting Staten Island, N.Y., from New Jersey. Manning the motorboat's helm is Andrew Willner, the newly designated watchdog of New York Harbor's waterways. A robust man with a salt-and-pepper beard, he describes, with wide eyes, the task before him — to hunt down the polluters of the nation's most industrialized port.

Weaving around four-storey oil tankers and tugs lugging garbage barges, Willner maps the waterscape's edge: Here, smoke-spewing towers mark a petro-chemical complex; there, clusters of storage tanks herald Exxon's Bayway plant; a mile downstream, the brown hump of Fresh Kills, the world's largest landfill, stretches across the horizon.

This is the nation's industrial breadbasket, a place we depend on — though we'd prefer not to see it. To the untrained eye, it's a grim wasteland. Yet hidden among the ragged islands and marshy recesses between pipes and tubes are some of the most important feeding and nesting areas for wading birds on the East Coast.

Each spring, thousands of little blue herons and black crowned night herons, great egrets and cattle egrets, fly here from the Caribbean. In all, these wetlands and estuaries serve as nurseries for 145 species of fish, and shelter for 125 species of birds. "The birds are here because food like worms and fiddler crabs are here," Willner explains. "The food is here because there's oxygen in the water. And there's oxygen in the water because the water quality is improving."

For years, municipalities dumped raw sewage into the harbor, robbing the water of life-giving oxygen. Other contaminants lacing the harbor's sediments include high concentrations of lead, dioxin, and PCBs. In the 1960s, researchers tested the Arthur Kill's condition by lowering cages filled with minnow-like killifish into the water, and clocking the hours that passed before they died.

The Clean Water Act of 1972, requiring towns to curtail untreated-sewage discharges, helped the harbor's wildlife revive. By the mid-1970s, bird-watchers sighted the return of the long-legged wading birds. "The birds symbolize the extraordinary resiliency of this recovering resource," says Willner. "But there's a place where that resiliency stops."

Environmentalists worry that last year's three major oil spills, as well as 653 smaller spills, have imperiled the harbor's ecosystem. During 1990, 1,355,000 gallons of petroleum products stained the Arthur Kill and Kill van Kull with black, gooey tar balls.

Government inspectors, hampered by budget cuts, rarely check the harbor's oil tankers, refineries, and storage areas, says Willner. The shortage of inspectors, combined with last year's spate of accidents, spurred the New Jersey-based American Littoral Society to name Willner its first official baykeeper. "The laws are on the books, but they're not getting enforced," he says. "We're going to embarrass the [state-environmental] agencies into doing a better job."

Andrew Willner, 46, is a licensed captain who learned to sail on New Jersey's Navesink River. Like the millions who live by it, he once dismissed the harbor as little more than a dead sea ... until one day, he spotted a sturgeon swimming among some pilings at Staten Island's edge.

"I was shocked that something could live in that water," he recalls. "That fish really drove home the incredible contrast between the area's wildlife and its industrial sprawl. It made me decide to dedicate myself to improving the harbor's environment."

Willner joins a growing network of citizen enforcers patrolling such waterways as the San Francisco Bay, the Puget Sound, and parts of the Mississippi River. In the New York area, there's a Hudson Riverkeeper, a Long Island Soundkeeper, and a Delaware Riverkeeper. The New York Harbor Baykeeper ensures that New York and New Jersey's major coastal waters will be treated as a linked ecosystem, monitored by environmentalists who aren't hemmed by state lines.

Riverkeeper programs are empowered by provisions in the Clean Water Act and other environmental laws, which enable citizens to file lawsuits if government agencies aren't vigorously pursuing polluters. In one case, Willner discovered that the New Jersey Transit repair facility near the Hackensack Meadowlands was dumping its waste oil into an unlined pit, which was leaking into the Hackensack River and, in turn, into the harbor. He reported the violation to the New Jersey Department of Environmental Protection, and the Littoral Society slapped New Jersey Transit with a 60-day notice of its intent to sue.

Later, Willner went through the DEP's records and found that the agency had known about the violation since 1986 — but did nothing about it. Meanwhile, the waste oil continues to spill into the river. "Here we have an unattended oil leak, but the DEP just doesn't seem to care," says Willner. "The only way to get their attention is to find the polluter, figure out why the agency hasn't done anything about it, and sue."

Yet Willner believes the best way to effect long-term improvement is to bring people to the harbor, and the harbor to the classroom. By highlighting the harbor's resources and problems, he hopes to form a network of advocates who will act as the eyes and ears for the baykeeper program.

"If we could get 2,000 people out here, my job would go away very quickly," he says. "Unfortunately, I don't think that's going to happen real soon."
— *Bill Breen*

Our busy lives, our need or desire to get ahead—all of our seemingly important obligations—often pull us away from life's simple daily miracles. Staying aware of the purpose and meaning of things, remembering their interconnections and knowing that all of our actions have consequences is not easy. Yet these may be our most important tasks in becoming *shomrei adamah*. If we do not remember who we are and what our place is, the human tendency to become masters and controllers of our universe can get the better of us.

It takes practice to learn to "see" and value all of life, just as it takes practice to become a good athlete, musician, artist, doctor or student. Judaism provides us with a multitude of practices to help us remember our place in the web of nature. Our rabbis understood the human condition and the tendency toward arrogance. They provided us with a wide range of practices to keep us on track, in harmony with God's creation. Reciting *brachot* (blessings) is one such practice. *Brachot* remind us that ultimately we humans are not the ones in charge. *Brachot* remind us to stop and pay attention to the world around us at times when we might otherwise take things for granted. In this way, *brachot* can train our eyes and our minds and enrich our lives.

•Participants will understand where *brachot* and giving thanks fit into the Jewish way of life, and how they are basic to an ecological perspective.
•Participants will have an opportunity to express their thanks for an aspect of creation.

•A loaf of bread or *challah*.
•Copies of Readings & Worksheets
•Paper and fine-point markers.

Blessings and Praise

Opening ▲

Invite participants to say the blessing over the bread with you. Break the bread and share it.

ברוך אתה ד׳ אלקינו מלך העולם המוציא לחם מן הארץ.

Baruch Atah Adonai Eloheynu Melech Ha-olam ha-mo-tzi lehem min ha-aretz.

Praise to You *Adonai*, our God and Universal Ruler, Who brings forth bread from the earth.

DISCUSSION QUESTIONS

•What is the purpose of *brachot* ?
Brachot *are a Jewish way of telling us to slow down and pay attention—something special is happening that we don't want to miss. Brachot can help us to know our place in the universe and to know that God has given everything a purpose (whether or not we are aware of that purpose).*

Brachot *are a momentary pause between the awareness of an act and the act itself. From a naturalist perspective, this pause may be considered unnatural; animals do not contemplate their food before eating. In this way brachot remind us of our humanity, and the distinctions between humans and the animal world.*

Have a volunteer read the selection from *God in Search of Man* by Abraham Joshua Heschel (see Readings & Worksheets). Rabbi Abraham Joshua Heschel was a modern theologian and important Jewish thinker who taught at the Jewish Theological Seminary. He wrote numerous books and was renowned for his work in the civil rights movement.

• Have you ever looked at *brachot* in the same way that Heschel does?

• Do you agree with Heschel? Could you imagine any change in your life if you looked differently at *brachot*?

• According to the *Talmud* (*Brachot* 35), "Man may not take pleasure in [or derive benefit from] any worldly thing until he has recited a blessing over it. Anyone who takes pleasure [or derives benefit] from this world without making a blessing is guilty of misappropriating sacred property [a sin punishable by death]." What does this mean?
Everything in nature is a gift from God; it does not belong to us. If we use something of nature without thanking God, we are, in effect, stealing. Giving thanks is our way of recognizing the Creator who gave us the gift.

• Can you think of traditions similar to *brachot* in any other cultures or religions, in which giving back to the earth is considered of critical importance?
Native American tradition: One always utters thanks when using anything from nature.

• Many people may have had the wonderful and important experience of noticing how magnificent or beautiful a tree is. Is there a difference between saying, "Oh wow, nice tree," and "Praise to You, God, who has created the trees"?
Both are personal expressions that praise and honor the life of the tree. One uses the Jewish vehicle for praise and appreciation, but both exclamations may stem from the same intentions.

Text Study: The *Brachot* ▲▲

There is a whole set of *brachot* which are less familiar to many Jews. These *brachot* are recited when a person experiences various natural phenomena.

After the Bible was written, the early rabbis interpreted and expanded upon the biblical laws. Around 200 C.E., Rabbi Judah the Prince collected all the Rabbis' discussions and interpretations of the Bible's laws and wrote them down in a book called the *Mishnah*.

It is in the *Mishnah* that we will find the roots of the *brachot* we say today. It is traditional for Jews to study the *Mishnah* in pairs called *Hevrutot* (sing. *Hevrutah*). Participants will study a selection from the first *masechet* (division): *Brachot* (Blessings), of the first *seder* (order): *Zeraim* (Seeds) 9:2.

Divide the group into *Hevrutah* pairs and hand out copies of the text and questions (see Readings & Worksheets). Allow ten minutes to study the texts and answer the questions. Regroup and discuss the texts, using the questions as a guide.

POINTS TO EMPHASIZE

By giving us these *brachot* to recite, the *Mishnah* is training us to appreciate the wonders of the daily world that have become commonplace to most of us.

Through the *brachot,* the *Mishnah* is teaching us of God's presence in nature—even in the frightening, powerful aspects of nature.

Many people feel closest to God outdoors; that is why we have a custom of putting windows in our synagogues. For some of us, praying indoors feels unnatural; we prefer the mountains for our temples.

Athletes, artists and musicians all exercise to improve their skills. *Brachot* are spiritual exercises that we can do to help us remember the source and the Eternal in everything. Reciting *brachot* can expand our appreciation and joy in life. With an expanded awareness of the inherent value of all life, can we still exploit the earth?

Your Own *Brachot* and Praises ▲▲

The Jewish people did not stop composing *brachot* after the *Mishnah* was compiled. Like Rabbi Judah, many sages believed that some natural phenomena were special enough to merit a new, unique *brachah* (sing. for *brachot*).

Examples of these post-*Mishnaic brachot* include:

•The blessing over a rainbow, the sign of God's covenant with Noah:

ברוך אתה ד׳ אלקינו מלך העולם זוכר הברית ונאמן בבריתו וקים במאמרו.

Baruch Atah Adonai Eloheynu Melech ha-olam, zocher ha-brit v'neeman b'vreeto v'kayam b'mamaro.

Praise to You *Adonai*, our God and Universal Ruler, Who remembers the covenant and keeps its promise faithfully with all creation.

•The blessing over fruit trees in bloom in Spring (this may be recited only once a year):

ברוך אתה ד׳ אלקינו מלך העולם שלא חסר בעולמו דבר וברא בו בריות טובות ואילנות טובים להנות בהם בני אדם.

Baruch Atah Adonai, Eloheynu Melech Ha-olam, she'lo chiser ba'olamo davar, oobarah bo briyot tovot v'eelanot tovim, l'hanot bahem b'nai adam.

Praise to You *Adonai*, our God and Universal Ruler, Who created a universe lacking in nothing, and who has fashioned goodly creatures and trees that give people pleasure.

Brachot are one way in which the Rabbis taught us to honor nature and God. Can you think of others?

The following story is told of Rabbi Nachman of Bratslav. He was raised in a city and never spent time in a natural setting until he was married (at age 14) and went to live with his wife in her village. Her village was in the midst of a beautiful countryside, and when he first got there, he couldn't believe how wonderful it felt to be in nature. He felt that outside, he could easily pray and talk to God. There was no one to bother him, and all the animals and plants helped his prayers reach heaven. He spent much time outdoors. When he became a rabbi, he told his congregants to spend one hour a day outdoors to commune with God. Have a volunteer recite Rabbi Nachman's prayer (see Readings & Worksheets).

Ask participants to also create their own *brachot and prayers*. Have them choose a part of nature for which they would like to compose a *brachah* or poem (for example: thunder, snowstorms, an eclipse, clouds, flowers, bird songs).

If it is to be a *brachah,* it should begin with the words "Praise to You *Adonai*, our God and Universal Ruler". Tell the class to think about how the part of nature they have chosen makes them think and feel about God. The *brachah* can be simple ("Praise to You, Adonai . . . Who makes grasshoppers") or more elaborate ("Praise to You, Eternal . . . Who creates flying insects that sing in the summer night"). The *brachot* should say something about God's presence in nature. Encourage participants to use a name for God that speaks to them, like "Eternal" or "Source of Life," and so on.

Brachot Sheets ▲▲

Hand out paper and fine-point markers. Have participants write their newly-created *brachot* and prayers along with some of the traditional *brachot* we have discussed. Encourage them to decorate their *"brachot* sheets" with drawings and designs.

[Note: According to some traditional Jewish legal teachings, it is no longer permissible to create our own *brachot*. If you take this stance, explore this and talk about the possible rationale for this position. Then, go ahead and have participants write on their sheets and illustrate them, using the traditional *brachot* only.]

Bringing It Home ▲

Brachot help us see God as part of everything in the world. When we view nature as connected with God we are less likely to mistreat or destroy it. Rabbi Meir said that "it is a *mitzvah* (commandment) to recite 100 blessings every day" (Babylonian *Talmud, Menahot* 43b). Could this help you in your life today? Is it appropriate to expect people to do this? Would it make a difference in the world if people did this? Try to notice the number of times a day you feel appreciation for anything. How do you feel when you are appreciative? What does it feel like on a day when you forget to appreciate things? It takes work to be conscious of your world and to be appreciative of it. Try over the next week to bless things in whatever way is comfortable to you. Compare notes next time and see if the work pays off.

For Further Reading

Abraham Joshua Heschel, *God in Search of Man*.

Blessings and Praise

Opening: From Abraham Joshua Heschel, God In Search of Man, pp. 48-51.

Reading

> Three times a day we pray:
>> We Thank Thee. . .
>> For Thy miracles which are daily with us,
>> For thy continual marvels. . .
> In the evening liturgy we recite the words of Job (9:10):
>> Who does great things past finding out,
>> Marvelous things without number.

Every evening we recite: "He creates light and makes the dark." Twice a day we say: "He is One." What is the meaning of such repetition? A scientific theory, once it is announced and accepted, does not have to be repeated twice a day. The insights of wonder must be constantly kept alive. Since there is a need for daily wonder, there is a need for daily worship.

The sense for the "miracles which are daily with us," the sense for the "continual marvels," is the source of prayer. There is no worship, no music, no love, if we take for granted the blessings or defeats of living. No routine of the social, physical, or physiological order must dull our sense of surprise at the fact that there *is* a social, a physical, or a physiological order. We are trained in maintaining our sense of wonder by uttering a prayer before the enjoyment of food. Each time we are about to drink a glass of water, we remind ourselves of the eternal mystery of creation, "Blessed be Thou. . . by Whose word all things come into being." A trivial act and a reference to the supreme miracle. Wishing to eat bread or fruit, to enjoy a pleasant fragrance or a cup of wine; on tasting fruit in season for the first time; on seeing a rainbow, or the ocean; on noticing trees when they blossom; on meeting a sage in Torah or in secular learning; on hearing good or bad tidings — we are taught to invoke His great name and our awareness of Him. Even on performing a physiological function we say "Blessed be Thou. . . who healest all flesh and *doest wonders*."

This is one of the goals of the Jewish way of living: to experience commonplace deeds as spiritual adventures, to feel the hidden love and wisdom in all things.

. . . The belief in "the hidden miracles is the basis for the entire Torah. A man has no share in the Torah, unless he believes that all things and all events in the life of the individual as well as in the life of society are miracles. There is no such thing as the natural course of events. . . ." (Nachmanides).

Blessings and Praise

Text Study: The *Brachot*: Mishnah Brachot 9:2

Reading

A. Upon seeing shooting stars, earthquakes, lightning, thunder, and storms, one says:

ברוך אתה ד׳ אלקינו מלך העולם שכחו וגבורתו מלא עולם.

Baruch ... she'kocho oog'voortoh maleh olam.
Praise to You... Whose strength and power fill the entire world.

B. Upon seeing mountains, valleys, oceans, rivers, and wilderness, one says:

ברוך אתה ד׳ אלקינו מלך העולם עשה בראשית.

Baruch... oseh breisheet.
Praise to You... making Creation work.

C. Rabbi Yehudah taught: One who sees the Great Sea (the Mediterranean) very rarely says:

ברוך אתה ד׳ אלקינו מלך העולם שעשה את הים הגדול.

Baruch... she'asah et ha-yam ha-gadol.
Praise to You...Who made the Great Sea.

D. Over rain and over good news, one says:

ברוך אתה ד׳ אלקינו מלך העולם הטוב והמטיב.

Baruch... ha-tov v'ha-mateev.
Praise to You... Who is Good and does Goodness.

1. What do the items in section A have in common? What do the items in section B have in common? How do the items in section A differ from those in section B?

2. Are the blessings in sections A and B appropriate for the items over which they are said? What do the blessings make us think about in each case? Why do you think the Rabbis chose these blessings for these items?

3. What items could you add to the lists in sections A and B?

4. Even though we already have a blessing for oceans, in section C, Rabbi Judah assigns the Great Sea its own *brachah*. Why do you think he does this? Are there any events or parts of nature that you believe deserve their own special blessing? Why?

5. Why do you think the blessing for rain is the same as the one for good news, and not the one for storms and thunder? This blessing would make a great deal of sense in a time of drought; should we still recite it in a time of flood?

6. Why do you think the *Mishnah* instructs someone who sees these things every day not to recite the blessing each time?

7. If we observed this tradition and recited blessings on a regular basis, how might it change the way we looked at the world around us?

8. Based on these blessings, the Rabbis seem to feel that when we look closely enough, every part of nature tells us something about God (examples: God's power, God's creative force). How might looking at nature in this way change the way we treat the natural world?

Blessings and Praise

Text Study: The *Brachot*: Mishnah Brachot 9:2

Leader Worksheet

1. What do the items in section A have in common? What do the items in section B have in common? How do the items in section A differ from those in section B?
All the items in section A are powerful, even frightening or destructive events. They are not everyday occurrences. The items in section B are common but beautiful, natural features. These items are constant-so constant that we often take them for granted.

2. Are the blessings in sections A and B appropriate for the items over which they are said? What do the blessings make us think about in each case? Why do you think the Rabbis chose these blessings for these items?
Yes. In the first case, the blessing speaks of God's power and in the second, the blessing speaks of evidence of God's amazing creativity. The first section's items are powerful and even frightening. They might seem to represent God's power. The second list of items might not seem special until we remember that God made them.

3. What items could you add to the lists in sections A and B?
A: volcanic eruptions; tidal waves; an eclipse
B: flowers; rocks; waterfalls

4. Even though we already have a blessing for oceans, in section C, Rabbi Judah assigns the Great Sea its own *brachah*. Why do you think he does this? Are there any events or parts of nature that you believe deserve their own special blessing? Why?
The Mediterranean had a special importance and meaning in the life of the Jewish people; it is the largest body of water close to the land of Israel. In the ancient world, the Mediterranean helped to define the boundaries of the "known" world.

5. Why do you think the blessing for rain is the same as the one for good news, and not the one for storms and thunder? This blessing would make a great deal of sense in a time of drought; should we still recite it in a time of flood?
As we all know (although we may not appreciate it all the time), rain is good news, providing sustenance for the crops, insuring that our tables will be full. What could be better than the knowledge that we will be able to eat another meal, and will be able to experience another day!! In the ancient Middle East, as well as in many parts of the world today, rain was unpredictable and often scarce. During a time of floods, we can pray for gentle, nourishing rains instead of destructive torrents.

6. Why do you think the *Mishnah* instructs someone who sees these things every day not to recite the blessing each time?
If one recited the same blessing every day, it could become rote and meaningless. Someone who has never seen the mountains or ocean before will undoubtedly be impressed on first viewing them.

7. If we observed this tradition and recited blessings on a regular basis, how might it change the way we looked at the world around us?

We may notice more, we may appreciate the beauties of nature more, we may be more careful about preserving the natural world, and we may feel closer to God more often.

8. Based on these blessings, the Rabbis seem to feel that when we look closely enough, every part of nature tells us something about God (examples: God's power, God's creative force). How might looking at nature in this way change the way we treat the natural world?

We would see the world as holy (connected with God) and therefore treat it with more respect and concern.

Blessings and Praise

Your Own *Brachot* and Praises: Rabbi Nachman's Prayer

Reading

Master of the Universe, grant me the ability to be alone:

May it be my custom to go outdoors each day, among the trees and grasses, among all growing things, there to be alone and enter into prayer.

There may I express all that is in my heart, talking with You, to Whom I belong.

And may all grasses, trees and plants awake at my coming.

Send the power of their life into my prayer, making whole my heart and my speech through the life and spirit of growing things.

Judaism and ecological thought have a strong parallel in their core

understanding of interrelationship and interdependence of everything in the

universe. Central to an understanding of ecology is the recognition of highly

interdependent networks of living things. Central to Judaism is an

understanding that all of our actions have repercussions. Both perspectives see

humans inextricably bound in the web of life. The goal of this lesson is to

explore the "web" that ties all living things, from both a Jewish and an

ecological perspective.

OBJECTIVES

•Participants will describe how the diverse parts of an ecosystem work together and depend on each other.
•Participants will recognize their personal significance as a part of the world community.
•Participants will discuss the Jewish spiritual significance of the ecological concept of interconnectedness.

MATERIALS & PREPARATION

•Copies of Jewish texts on interconnectedness for each pair of participants.(See Readings & Worksheets)
•Four large sheets of butcher paper; markers for each group. (If you cannot get butcher paper, make a large sheet of paper by cutting open several paper bags so that they lie flat. Cut and tape them together, overlapping the edges about one inch. Turn the sheet over for use.)
•A copy of *Chad Gadya* can be found in any Passover *Haggadah*. Depending on your audience you may want to bring in an Aramaic, transliterated and/or English-language version.

Web of Life

Interconnections and Interdependence ▲

Have the participants list some commonly purchased items such as jeans, sneakers, a loaf of bread, a hamburger from a fast food place. Divide participants into 4 groups and have each group pick an item from the brainstormed list. Give each group a large piece of butcher paper and some markers.

Have the groups map out graphically the relationships between themselves and the origins of their items. Encourage the participants to imagine every detail of how the item came to them. Use the questions below to guide their thinking. You can write the questions on the board.

•What is the item made of? Where did the elements that make up the item come from?

•What chemicals and other resources are needed to develop the product?

•How much energy would it take to produce this product, from the beginning?

•How is it grown?

•How and where are people employed in the process? What do you imagine their lives are like?

•Does the process of making the item produce waste or pollution? What will become of the waste products?

•What impact might that waste have on the environment?

•Where would the waste products be released—near you, or somewhere else where others will have to deal with it?

•What are the points in the process that would require transportation in order for the item to reach you?

For example, if they picked a fast food hamburger, participants would need to imagine where the beef was raised. It may have come from South America; a rain forest may have been cleared to raise cattle for their hamburger. What happens to the soil when the trees are cut down? It is possible that the indigenous animals and people were displaced. Chemicals were probably used to keep the cattle healthy and fatten them. Then the cattle were probably transported to a feed lot, and after fattening, slaughtered. The meat had to be packaged and transported to a central point for the fast food chain, then distributed to their local outlet where it was cooked, requiring the expenditure of more energy. At every stage in this process people were doing their jobs. People in South America probably work for very low wages in very poor conditions. The people working in fast food chains probably do not earn enough to support themselves in expensive urban areas.

Tape the "maps" on the wall around the room so participants can think about them while they complete the rest of the "Web of Life."

Threads in the Web ▲

The maps (see previous activity) show a human-made web that affects both people and the environment. In nature, everything is interdependent and bound together in webs called ecosystems.

•What are some examples of interdependent relationships in ecosystems?

Examples: Flowers and pollinators—certain species of orchids have only one species of hummingbird as a pollinator, and the orchid is the sole source of food for the hummingbird. Every flower needs a pollinator to survive; every pollinator needs pollen to survive.

How are ecosystems affected by the loss or alteration of a plant, animal or other element?
The entire ecosystem is changed and perhaps even irrepairably damaged.

What follows below are two examples of the complexity of the web of life. (See Readings & Worksheets). Ask for volunteers to read these examples to the class.

1) The first selection is by Rachel Carson. Rachel Carson laid the foundation for environmental activism in America. Her book, *Silent Spring*, alerted the public to the consequences of environmental pollution, particularly pesticides. What follows is a classic example of what happens when the web of life is disturbed.

2) The second selection, Gefilte Fish Story, is by Dr. Gabriel Goldman. Dr. Goldman is the Director of Curriculum at the Cleveland Bureau of Education and is an avid fisherman and *shomer adamah.*

Text Study: Interconnectedness ▲▲

Jewish tradition also talks about the way diverse parts are interconnected in one complex system. Use the text sheets at the end of this lesson to study traditional Jewish views of interconnectedness.

Divide the group into *hevrutah*, study partners, and assign each pair a copy of the *Sh'ma*, and *one* text (numbered 1 through 9). There are ten readings including the *Sh'ma* (See Readings & Worksheets).

[Number 9 is a more difficult reading, which looks at the Gaia hypothesis. Gaia is the name ancient Greeks gave to the earth. The implication of the Gaia hypothesis is that the earth is one living organism. This is a radical position; the scientific method traditionally reduces nature to its component parts in order to understand it. You may want to point this out to participants and ask for a volunteer willing to tackle this reading.]

Each *hevrutah* pair will work on the *Sh'ma* and one other (numbered) reading. Give participants about ten minutes to work on their texts, answering the questions that go with their text. They will then regroup and discuss the *Sh'ma* first. The leader can use the discussion questions and answers as a guide. Next, each pair will read aloud its text and will present the significance of this text to the web of life. They will entertain questions from other participants. The leader may help guide the discussion, using the leader's worksheet (see Readings & Worksheets). Conclude by emphasizing that our sense of interconnectedness should lead us to express our concern for environmental issues and shape our everyday actions.

POINTS TO EMPHASIZE

We are part of many interconnected systems, from the interlocking systems of ourbodies to the web of life on earth. As a part of such systems, we are dependent upon and responsible for one another. Our daily bodily processes—just the fact that we are alive—have an impact on the atmosphere and every other part of the universe.

Our tradition speaks of God as the ultimate Unity, the Oneness that underlies the web of life. By saying that God is One (in the *Sh'ma*), we are, in a sense, saying that everything exists as a part of God—that God is "in" everything; God is the living, eternal force that binds us all.

As we have seen, Judaism and ecology both place great importance on the concept of interconnectedness—the web of life. If we are all connected, then we have a special obligation both as part of the human race and as Jews to take responsibility for the impact of our actions upon each other, plants and other animals.

Bringing It Home ▲

Rachel Carson describes the web of life at Clear Lake as "a house-that-Jack-built sequence." There is a song from the Jewish tradition that also describes a web of life. *Chad Gadya*, "One Little Goat [Kid]," was written in the Middle Ages and passed down in the Passover *Haggadah*. It is written in Aramaic. Pass out copies of the song If you know the tune, sing along! In some families there is even a tradition for different people to take on the various roles of the characters in the song and to make a role-appropriate sound each time their character is mentioned (God should play God's self). Think about the web spun between the animals and others in the song. The *kavannah* for the week is to be aware of how the actions that you take affect other people and ultimately the whole world.

For Further Reading

Rabbi Lawrence Kushner, "All Things are Connected" in *The Book of Miracles*.

Lewis Thomas, *The Lives of A Cell*.

Web of Life

Threads in the Web: Factual Source: Rachel Carson, *Silent Spring*, pp. 50-53.

Reading

In the early 1950's in Clear Lake, California, an annoying gnat occurred in tremendous numbers. Attepts to control it failed until DDD, a chemical insecticide related to DDT, came to the rescue. It was applied in very dilute amounts so that for every part of chemical there were 70 million parts water. At first the treatment controlled the gnats, but it had to be repeated in 1954, this time at 1 part to 50 million. At that time, it was believed that the gnats were completely eradicated.

Yet by the following winter it was clear that other forms of life were affected: the western grebes on the lake began to die. More than a hundred of them were reported dead. Following a third assault of DDD on the stubborn gnat population more grebes died. When someone thought to analyze the fatty tissues of the grebes, he found them loaded with DDD in the extraordinary concentration of 1600 parts per million.

How did this occur? These birds, of course, eat fish. Upon analyzing the Clear Lake fish the picture became clear. The poison was picked up by the smaller organisms, concentrated and passed up the line to the larger predators. Plankton organisms were found to contain about 5 parts per million of the insecticide (about 25 times the maximum concentration ever reached in the water); plant-eating fishes had built up accumulations ranging from 40 to 300 parts per million; carnivorous species had stored the most of all.... It was a "house-that-Jack-built" sequence, in which the large carnivores had eaten the smaller carnivores, that had eaten the herbivores, that had eaten the plankton, that had absorbed the poison from the water.

This web of poisoning, then, seems to rest on a base of tiny innocuous plants. What happens to the human at of the opposite end of the food chain?

So what could be so terrible about gefilte fish (literally "filled fish")? It has graced the *Shabbat* and holiday tables of European and American Jews for generations. Practically every Ashkenazi Jew has his or her favorite gefilte fish, a certain brand or Bubby's old-world recipe.

The time has come to de-mythologize the gefilte fish. The truth is, gefilte fish was always a "poor man's" food, made from the cheapest and most plentiful fish. In Europe, that was carp, a fresh-water fish inhabiting most streams and lakes. To understand the potential problem with gefilte fish today, one must understand the nature of water pollution and the behavioral characteristics of carp, still a major ingredient in homemade and commercial brands of gefilte fish.

Carp are bottom eaters. They laze on the floors of rivers and lakes, sucking up particles of food that have dropped down. Their mouths are well suited for this task, shaped like flexible vacuum cleaner hoses. And they are not particular about what they eat. Carp bait includes just about anything—hot dogs, blood sacks, bubble gum, dough balls and cow liver. Fishermen have dubbed carp "pigs of the sea" and few outdoorsmen would consider eating them.

The problem is that carp suck up more than just the food they eat. They also suck up mud and other sediments, including toxic waste and pollutants which have settled to the bottom over the years. Most of these toxins and heavy metals cannot be eliminated from the system of organisms ingesting them.

The large majority of carp used in commercial gefilte fish are caught in the Detroit River, a highly polluted body of water that supplies 90 percent of the water in Lake Erie. In 1990, the Michigan Department of Natural Resources declared all Michigan lakes polluted and recommended not eating the fish caught in them. Likewise, Ohio has issued warnings against eating carp and catfish from Lake Erie. In fact, due to carp contamination, Ohio banned their commercial sales in the state. However, commercial fishermen can sell their Lake Erie carp and catfish catches out of state. Much of the carp is sold to New York gefilte fish companies.

Even gefilte fish made from carp raised on special fish "farms" in the mid-West and East cannot be considered safe without testing. Unlike the Great Lakes, these farms are not subjected to direct waste disposal, but they are still subject to airborne pollution. Factory pollutants can travel hundreds of miles to contaminate water with toxins.

Every day it seems like another agency or organization is finding something unhealthy about the foods we most enjoy. Health warnings have become so commonplace that it is easier and easier for us to ignore them. The case against consuming carp and gefilte fish, however, is crystal clear; eat carp and run the risk of ingesting pollutants and toxins that can never be eliminated from your body. Recommending that gefilte fish, as it is presently made, should not be a part of our festive tables may be "heresy," but it is also a matter of health.

Text Study: Interconnectedness: The *Sh'ma*, Deuteronomy 11:13-21

Reading

If you will listen to my *mitzvot* — which I will instruct you about today — toward love of your God and serving God with all your heart and all your spirit...then I will give the dew of your land in its season — the early and the late rains; you will gather your new grain, wine and oil. I will give grass in your field for your domestic animals; you will eat and be satisfied. Be attentive that your hearts are not tempted so that you turn away, serve and bow to other gods. God will be angry with you, and God will stop the heavens and withhold rain — and the earth will not yield its produce; you will be quickly loosed from the good land which God is giving you. Put My words on your heart and in your spirit, knot them on your hand as a sign; let them be bands between your eyes. Teach your children to recite them — when you settle down in your home, when you walk on a path, when you lie down and when you get up. Write them on the doorposts of your house and gate is so that you and your children will live a long time on the earth which God swore to give your ancestors like days of heaven on earth.

Web of Life

Text Study: Interconnectedness

Readings

1. Praise to You *Adonai*, our God and Universal Ruler, who — in partnership with Wisdom — formed and created crevices and channels within humankind; it is shown and known in front of Your honorable throne that if one of them were to be [inappropriately] opened or closed, it would be impossible to continue facing You, even for a single hour. Praise to You *Adonai*, Healer of all flesh, inspiring in what You can do.
—Prayerbook, morning blessings.

2. But the Holy One, blessed be He—may His great name be blessed forever and to all eternity!—in His wisdom and understanding created the whole world, created the heavens and the earth, the beings on high and those down below, and formed in man whatever He created in His world:

He created forests in the world and He created forests in man: to wit, man's hair;
He created channels in the world and He created channels in man: to wit, man's ears;
He created a wind in the world and He created a wind in man: to wit, man's breath;
A sun in the world and a sun in man: to wit, man's forehead. . .
Salt water in the world and salt water in man: to wit, man's tears. . .
Towers in the world and towers in man: to wit, man's neck;
Masts in the world and masts in man: to wit, man's arms;
Pegs in the world and pegs in man: to wit, man's fingers. . .
Millstones in the world and millstones in man: to wit, man's stomach. . .
Flowing waters in the world and flowing waters in man: to wit, man's blood . . .
Trees in the world and trees in man: to wit, man's bones. . .
Pestle and mortar in the world and pestle and mortar in man: to wit, man's joints. . .
Horses in the world and horses in man: to wit, man's legs. . .
Thus thou dost learn that whatever the Holy One, blessed be He, created in His world, He created in man.
—From *The Fathers According to Rabbi Nathan*, pp. 127-28.

3. May s/he [the deceased] be bound up in the bond of life.
—From the traditional *Yizkor* and funeral prayer.

4. One glorious chain of love, of giving and receiving, unites all creatures. None is by or for itself, but all things exist in continual reciprocal activities—the One for the all and the all for the One. None has power, or means for itself; each receives only in order to give, and gives in order to receive and finds therein the purpose of existence.
—S.R. Hirsch, *The Nineteen Letters of Ben Uzziel*, p.36.

5. One generation leaves, another arrives,
But the earth remains the same forever.
The sun rises, and the sun sets —
And hastens to the place where it arose.
The wind goes toward the south and turns north,
turning and turning it goes and returns full circle;
All streams flow to the sea,
Yet the sea is never full;
To the place from which they flow
The streams flow back again.
All words exhaust a person's ability to speak;
The eye can never see enough, the ear can never hear enough.
The thing that has been, it is what will be;
And that which is done is that which will be done,
And there is nothing new under the sun.
—Ecclesiastes 1:4-9

6. By the sweat of your brow you will eat your bread, until you return to the ground
— for from it you were taken. For dust you are, and to dust you shall return.
—Genesis 3:19

7. One of the marvels of early Wisconsin was the Round River, a river that flowed into itself, and thus sped around and around in a never-ending circuit. . . Wisconsin not only had a round river, Wisconsin is one. The current is the stream of energy which flows out of the soil into plants, thence into animals, thence back into the soil in a never ending circuit of life.
—Aldo Leopold, *A Sand County Almanac*, p.188.

8. The Power of the World always works in circles and everything tries to be round. . . The sky is round and I have heard that the earth is round like a ball and so are the stars. The wind in its greatest power, whirls. Birds make their nest in circles, for theirs is the same religion as ours. The sun comes forth and goes down again in a circle. The moon does the same, and both are round. Even the seasons form a great circle in their changing, and always come back again to where they were. The life of a man is a circle from childhood to childhood, and so it is in everything where power moves.
—John Neihardt, *Black Elk Speaks*, pp.198-199.

9. The actual stability of the atmosphere can best be understood by assuming that the atmosphere is actively and sensitively maintained by the oceans, the soils, the plants and the creatures — indeed, by the whole of the biosphere. In James Lovelock's words,

"The hypothesis states that the entire range of living matter on earth, from whales to viruses and from oaks to algae, could be regarded as constituting a single living entity, capable of manipulating the Earth's atmosphere to suit its overall needs and endowed with faculties and powers far beyond those of its constituent parts."

It is significant that the first evidence that the surface of this planet functions as a living entity should come from a study of the atmosphere, the very aspect of the Earth that we most commonly forget. The air is so close to us that we tend to leave it out of our thinking entirely—much as we do not attend to the experience of breathing, an act so essential to our existence that we take it for granted. The air that surrounds us is invisible to our eyes; doubtless this has something to do with why we usually act and speak as though there were nothing there.

The air can no longer be confused with mere negative presence or with the absence of solid things. . . . We are immersed in its depths as surely as fish are immersed in the sea. In concert with other animals, the plants, and with the microbes themselves, we're an active part of the earth's atmosphere, constantly circulating the breath of this planet through our brains and bodies, exchanging certain vital gases for others, and thus monitoring and maintaining the delicate make-up of the medium. As Lovelock has indicated, the methane produced by the microorganisms that make their home in our digestive tracts—the gas we produce in our guts— may conceivably be one of our essential contributions to the dynamic stability of the atmosphere (less important, to be sure, than the methane contribution of ruminant animals, but essential nonetheless).
—David Abram, *The Perceptual Implications of Gaia*, p.7.

Web of Life

Text Study: Interconnectedness

Participant Worksheet

Background

The first text is from Deuteronomy 11:13-21; it is also found in the prayerbook; it is the second paragraph of the *Sh'ma*. It draws a distinct connection between human behavior and the fate of the natural world. Those of us who follow a practice of Jewish prayer say it every day.

The first numbered text is from the prayerbook. It is a *brachah* that, traditionally, the Jew says every morning after going to the washroom. The second text was written by Rabbi Nathan between 200-700 C.E. The third text comes from the end of a prayer that is recited at every Jewish funeral, over the deceased. The fourth text comes from a book by a nineteenth-century Orthodox rabbi named Samson Raphael Hirsch. The fifth and sixth texts are both biblical, from Genesis and Ecclesiastes respectively. The seventh text is from Aldo Leopold's *A Sand County Almanac*. We discussed Aldo Leopold in the unit on "Seeing." The eighth text is by Black Elk, a Native American spokesperson. The ninth is a text within a text. The inner text is from James Lovelock, the contemporary scientist who established the "Gaia hypothesis." The outer text is by David Abram, a nature writer and ecophilosopher who has been very active with *Shomrei Adamah*.

DISCUSSION QUESTIONS

•On a simple level, God promises to reward us with rain and ample harvests if we are good. But do you see another way to read the *Sh'ma,* relating it to ecological concerns?

•Likewise, the Deuteronomy text declares that if we forsake God and turn to false gods, the rains will stop, the earth will not yield its produce, and we will be exiled. How might an ecology-minded Jew read this verse?

1) The morning prayer (text #1) speaks of the interconnectedness of all the parts of our body into one balanced network (and praises God for creating and sustaining the marvelous system that is the body). Can you think of any examples of how one malfunctioning part of the body affects other parts?

2) The second text demonstrates another example of the web of life. What does it teach about the web?

3) Remembering the concept of the "web of life", why do you think we ask that one who has just died become a part of that web?

4) Hirsch speaks indirectly of the web of life when he refers to the one chain that unites all creatures. He goes on, however, to relate the unity of all creatures to the oneness of God (The One). How do you think God is related to the web of life?

5) A different web of life is described in the Ecclesiastes selection. What is this web?

6) How are humans part of the web?

7) What does Aldo Leopold mean when he calls Wisconsin a river?

8) Does Black Elk's message remind you of any of the Jewish texts here?

9) Is James Lovelock's "Gaia hypothesis" teaching us anything different from what we've already learned in the other texts?

Web of Life

Text Study: Interconnectedness

Leader Worksheet

Background

The first text is from Deuteronomy 11:13-21; it is also found in the prayerbook; it is the second paragraph of the *Sh'ma*. It draws a distinct connection between human behavior and the fate of the natural world. Those of us who follow a practice of Jewish prayer say it every day.

The first numbered text is from the prayerbook. It is a *brachah* that, traditionally, the Jew says every morning after going to the washroom. The second text was written by Rabbi Nathan between 200-700 C.E. The third text comes from the end of a prayer that is recited at every Jewish funeral, over the deceased. The fourth text comes from a book by a nineteenth-century Orthodox rabbi named Samson Raphael Hirsch. The fifth and sixth texts are both biblical, from Genesis and Ecclesiastes respectively. The seventh text is from Aldo Leopold's *A Sand County Almanac*. We discussed Aldo Leopold in the unit on "Seeing." The eighth text is by Black Elk, a Native American spokesperson. The ninth is a text within a text. The inner text is from James Lovelock, the contemporary scientist who established the Gaia hypothesis. The outer text is by David Abram, a nature writer and ecophilosopher who has been very active with *Shomrei Adamah*.

DISCUSSION QUESTIONS

•On a simple level, God promises to reward us with rain and ample harvests if we are good. But do you see another way to read the *Sh'ma*, relating it to ecological concerns?
Given the current concerns about global warming, desertification and other environmental problems, one could understand that obeying God implies conserving energy, refraining from using polystyrene and CFCs, recycling—and the reward for doing so will be a livable planet.

•Likewise, the Deuteronomy text declares that if we forsake God and turn to false gods, the rains will stop, the earth will not yield its produce, and we will be exiled. How might an ecology-minded Jew read this verse?
One might understand "false gods" to refer to destructive technology, human greed and other vices that harm our planet and threaten to leave us "exiled," without a healthy home for ourselves and the rest of creation.

1) The morning prayer (text #1) speaks of the interconnectedness of all the parts of our body into one balanced network (and praises God for creating and sustaining the marvelous system that is the body). Can you think of any examples of how one malfunctioning part of the body affects other parts?

Examples: a bad foot may cause someone to limp, which may, in turn, cause back trouble; shoulder pain may be the sign of a forthcoming heart attack; something you eat may cause an allergy in the skin. The body is a complex, interconnected system.

2) The second text demonstrates another example of the web of life. What does it teach about the web?
The world and its web are reflected in human beings.
In his Guide of the Perplexed, *Moses Maimonides speaks of humans as microcosms; small versions of the world. Our millions of cells and body parts can be compared to communities of plants and people, our veins and arteries to great rivers, etc.*

3) Remembering the concept of the "web of life," why do you think we ask that one who has just died become a part of that web?
Perhaps the funeral prayer refers to the web of eternal life—an after-life. On the other hand, it may also refer to the fact that death does not remove us from the web of life in this world (although it does change our place in that web). After we die, our remains provide nutrients for the soil, from which a tree may grow, which provides a home to an owl, and so forth. Thus we remain, even in our death, very much a part of the web of life.

4) Hirsch speaks indirectly of the web of life when he refers to the one chain that unites all creatures. He goes on, however, to relate the unity of all creatures to the oneness of God (The One). How do you think God is related to the web of life?
This is a difficult question. But clearly God's oneness is a very important tenet of Judaism—consider the Sh'ma. *It could be said that by being the One, God is the ultimate connection, the sum total of all the threads that make up the web of life.*

5) A different web of life is described in the Ecclesiastes selection. What is this web?
It is the cycle of inorganic elements-the rivers, the water cycle, the wind, the earth, the sun. All elements, organic and inorganic, are connected in a web, a grand cycle of life.

6) How are humans part of the web?
We are made of the same organic elements that are in the soil, and when we die, we decompose back to the elements. Our bodies go back to the place from which we came.

7) What does Aldo Leopold mean when he calls Wisconsin a river?
The Round River is a major geological feature of Wisconsin. Through it flow all elements as they go through various phases of life, death and decomposition. The river provides energy for all life processes and affects the climate. By depositing sediments, it has an effect on land formations.

8) Does Black Elk's message remind you of any of the Jewish texts here?
It is reminiscent of the quotation from Ecclesiastes. Note the similarities and differences between the two.

9) Is James Lovelock's "Gaia hypothesis" teaching us anything different from what we've already learned in the other texts?

He's giving scientific basis to the interdependence of all life. Through his work, we are more aware of the atmosphere as a real entity, rather than just empty space. We see the atmosphere as more alive, subjected to all the life processes and adapting to them. We see the earth as one organism, made up of interdependent parts.

Humans are guests on earth; God is our host. We are part of the web of life, and

simultaneously, we have a unique task: the responsibility to preserve this

beautiful gift of the earth for the next generation. This responsibility is a part of

what it means to be human. For Jews, caring for the earth is our birthright and

responsibility: we need only remember the most intimate relationship between

adam (earthling) and *adamah* (earth).

The goal of this lesson is to demonstrate how a Jewish law, *bal tashchit*, "Do

Not Destroy", is applicable to the contemporary environmental crisis.

•Participants will be able to articulate the law of *bal tashchit* and its rabbinic genesis.
•Participants will examine their own behaviors in terms of *bal tashchit*. and will learn to decrease the waste in their lives.

MATERIALS & PREPARATION

• Bring the following for the Opening exercise: Paper bag, a sandwich wrapped in plastic, soda can or foil, some pre-packaged food like chips, juice pack and a sample of an unpackaged food like an apple.
•Each group member should bring in one item of what they normally consider garbage.
•Art supplies including glue, paints, glitter.
•Copies of Readings & Worksheets.
•Speak to your institution's administrators and ascertain whether your group may perform an environmental audit (see "Detective Work").

Bal Tashchit

Opening ▲

Our American society is the most wasteful society in the history of humanity. The value of the resources that we throw away is higher than the GNP (Gross National Product) of many other countries. In the average American's lifetime, he or she will throw out 45 tons of garbage. The problem of garbage is worsened by our inadequate means of disposal. Most landfills are filling up fast, and other means, such as incineration, are not considered environmentally sound. Waste reduction through the use of the three R's, **R**educe waste, **R**euse products and **R**ecycle, is considered the intelligent way to approach the waste problem.

Take out a paper lunch bag filled with what would be a typical lunch and proceed to take out each item. The lunch should contain the following types of items:

Paper: the bag itself
Plastic: a sandwich wrapped in plastic
Aluminum: soda can or foil
Packaged food: chips, juice pack
Unpackaged food: fruit

Take out each food item and the packaging associated with it.

Where does plastic come from, and where does it go after lunch is over? Repeat this question for each of the the items in the lunch.

•Plastic: Every year 50 billion pounds of plastic are made in the United States (see "The Path of Plastic" in Readings & Worksheets).

•Aluminum: Every three months we throw away enough aluminum to replace all the commercial airplanes in the U.S.

•Paper: The paper equivalent of 500,000 trees is used every Sunday to print the Sunday paper in the U.S.

•Packaged food: Thirty-three percent of our garbage is just unnecessary packaging.

Text Study: The Law of *Bal Tashchit* ▲▲

There are two concerns about waste expressed in Deuteronomy. Ask volunteers to read the following passages:

"There will be an area beyond the military camp where you can relieve yourself. You will have a spade among your weapons; and after you have squatted, you will dig a hole and cover your excrement."
—Deuteronomy 23:13-15

"When you lay seige and battle against a city for a long time in order to capture it, you *must not destroy* its trees, wielding an ax against them. You may eat of them, but you must not cut them down. Are the trees of the field human to withdraw before you into the besieged city? Only trees which you know do not yield food may be destroyed; you may cut them down for constructing siege works against the city that is waging war on you, until it has been captured."
—Deuteronomy 20:19-20

DISCUSSION QUESTIONS

•The first passage is rather explicit. Are you surprised to hear such things in the Bible? How does this law make you feel (do you find it repulsive, fascinating, etc.)?
Judaism is concerned with all aspects of life in this world. One of the beauties of the tradition is its attention to the small details we often take for granted.

•The second passage is more difficult. We will be studying this in detail. What does this law mean?
In wartime we may eat from fruit trees, but are forbidden to cut them down. This law is referred to as Bal Tashchit.
In general, fruit trees serve no other purpose but to bear fruit. Compare fruit trees to other trees: oak, maple, cedar. These trees are much larger, and are solid. They are excellent for building. They could serve well to construct the siege works. Fruit trees, on the other hand, are not useful for building. They serve primarily to bear fruit. Animals and humans can benefit from the fruit. The Torah *is telling us we cannot cut down trees senselessly, simply for convenience, because we don't like them or because we want to harm the enemy. A scorched earth policy is forbidden according to the Bible. If not, it would be wasteful or destructive.*

The Rabbis used many different interpretive tools in order to understand the Bible. One tool is called *kal v' homer* (literally, from hard to easy). *Kal v'homer* means that we infer from a difficult situation how to behave in an easier situation. In other words, if you find one law in a specific biblical context the rabbis can extend its application to other related situations. An example of this is reciting a blessing before eating. The only blessing that we are commanded to make is the blessing after eating. The Rabbis reasoned that if we are commanded to recite a blessing after eating, when our appetite is satiated, when we are tired and do not feel compelled to make a blessing, then there is all the more reason to say a blessing before we have eaten, when we are eager to eat and making a blessing would be a simple act.

Deuteronomy 20:19-20 was extended to other situations based on the law of *kal v'homer*. In this activity, we'll be thinking about how we can apply *kal v'homer* to *bal tashchit*.

Divide the group into pairs. Hand out the text and questions on *bal tashchit* (see Readings & Worksheets). Have participants answer the questions, using the text study sheet as a reference. Reconvene after ten minutes and discuss the material using the study questions as a guide.

[Note: Leader may use current and local environmental issues for a more up-to-date and inspiring discussion.]

Garbage Art ▲▲▲

When you throw something away, where is "away"?

There is no such thing as "away." Garbage always goes somewhere. The only way to deal with the problem of garbage is through the three R's. To demonstrate how we can reduce the amount of waste by reusing what would normally go into the waste stream, the class will make an art project out of the waste items they have brought in with them.

What Do You Know About Waste? ▲

Ask participants to take the "What Do You Know Quiz" (see Readings & Worksheets). Go over answers. Participants will be astonished at how much we ourselves and our country waste or unnecessarily destroy.

Detective Work: Conducting an Audit of Your School or Institution ▲▲▲

Invite participants to be *bal tashchit* detectives and investigate where their institution wastes; submit suggestions to the administration to decrease waste. Begin this activity now. Participants will need to take on the responsibility to research more on their own. After hours or during lunch, participants could examine the trash generated in various offices and classrooms. Participants can give a booby prize to the greatest offenders, and an award to the most creative conserver.

Begin with a brainstorming session. Have a volunteer write on the blackboard, while participants offer suggestions of areas that use resources and produce waste. Ask for suggestions on how waste can be decreased in each area. If after brainstorming they have not come up with the following ideas, you can offer them.

•Do they recycle paper, plastics and metals? Check the packaging of the toilet paper and paper towels used. Is there a "recycled" label?

•Is recycled paper used for photocopying and office needs? Hold the paper up to the light; if it is recycled, there will probably be a watermark of the recycling sign.

•What is the volume of paper used for fliers and newsletters? Can it be consolidated? Are memos written on the backs of old letters?

•Does the institution use non-recyclable items? Can recyclables or reusables be substituted (for instance, cheap silverware instead of plastic throw-away eating utensils)? What is thrown away that can be reused or can be replaced with a recyclable alternative?

•What is the energy source of the institution? Are there alternatives? What is the usual heat setting? Are excess lights left on at night?

•How much energy is used? Can energy be reduced? What sort of light bulbs are used? How is the insulation?

•Is the institution making maximal use of its space? Are unused rooms heated? What happens in the space at night, and in the summer?

•What is the air conditioner's usual setting? Will a fan suffice? Are there trees planted around the facility that could cool the building, eliminating the need for air conditioning?

•Are carpooling, public transportation, or bike riding encouraged?

•Are cleaning supplies or lawn products toxic?

•What sort of toxics are thrown away? How are they disposed of?

•How much food is thrown away at events?

•Where does the waste water (dishwater) go?

At this point focus on a few of the items and come up with a plan on how the institution can follow *bal tashchit*.

When planning, be sure to:
•Choose a plan of action that the administration will allow
•Set a reasonable goal
•Determine how to measure waste
•Assign tasks to participants, and follow through with your plan!

Bringing It Home ▲

(This activity may be substituted for the audit if you feel it is more appropriate. Many of the same questions will apply.)

We must realize that we have the ability and power to make changes in the world. Good stewardship (caring for the earth) begins at home. Therefore the participants must look at their habits and the habits of their families to determine what needs to be changed. Spend a few minutes discussing participants' own personal habits in reference to *bal tashchit*. Discuss areas where they waste resources. Decide how they may be able to improve these behaviors and habits. Have participants perform a week-long project at home, recording everything that is thrown away or used up (such as gallons of gasoline for the cars, gallons of water for the lawn or garden, gallons of bathwater, gallons of toilet bowl water, gallons of dishwater). Encourage them to work out plans for following the commandment of *bal tashchit* at home.

For Further Reading

The Earthworks Group, *50 Simple Things You Can do to Save the Earth.*

Fossil fuels are the remains of plants and animals (organic matter) that died millions of years ago. Over the millennia, layers upon layers of sediment were deposited, compressing the remains with their enormous weight. Under this pressure, heat was generated. This heat, along with chemical and bacterial activity, gradually reformed the organic matter into the compounds of hydrogen and carbon we know as petroleum (when distilled, petroleum produces oil).

In order to obtain petroleum, the land must be "cleared": stripped of all plants and guarded against the return of indigenous animals. The land is then graded— bulldozed to accommodate derricks. Often roads must be built to make the area accessible to heavy equipment and workers. Sometimes a larger area is cleared in order to establish nearby housing for the oil field workers.

After the oil is pumped and shipped to a factory, chemicals and heat are added to transform it into plastic. The heat causes the molecules in oil to move around rapidly, and the chemicals cause the carbon molecules to bond in various formations. The fraction of carbon molecules that bond determines whether the plastic is hard or soft.

Text Study: The Law of *Bal Tashchit*

Readings

When in your war against a city you have to besiege it for a long time in order to capture it, you must not destroy its fruit trees, wielding an ax against them. You may eat of them, but you must not cut them down. Are the trees of the city human to withdraw from you into the besieged city? Only trees which you know do not yield food may be destroyed; you may cut them down for constructing siege works against the city that is waging war on you, until it has been captured.
—Deuteronomy 20:19-20

Whoever breaks vessels or rips up garments, destroys a building, stops up a fountain, or ruins food is guilty of violating the prohibition of *bal tashchit*.
—Babylonian *Talmud Kiddushin* 32a

It is forbidden to cut down fruit-bearing trees outside a [besieged] city, nor may a water channel be deflected from them so that they wither, as it is said: "You must not destroy its trees" [Deut. 20:19]. It [a fruit bearing tree] may be cut down, however, if it causes damage to other trees or to a field belonging to another man or if its value for other purposes is greater [than that of the fruit it produces]. The law forbids only wanton destruction.
—Maimonides, *Mishnah Torah*; Judges, Laws of Kings and Their Wars 6:8-10.

...[D]estruction does not only mean making something purposelessly unfit for its designated use; it also means trying to attain a certain aim by making use of more things and more valuable things when fewer and less valuable ones would suffice; or if this aim is not really worth the means expended for its attainment. [For example] kindling something which is still fit for other purposes for the sake of light;...wearing down something more than is necessary...consuming more than is necessary...

On the other hand, if destruction is necessary for a higher and more worthy aim, then it ceases to be destruction and itself becomes wise creating. [For example] cutting down a fruit tree which is doing harm to other more valuable plants, [and] burning a vessel when there is a scarcity of wood in order to protect one's weakened self from catching cold...
—Reprinted and adapted with permission of the publisher from Hirsch, Samson Raphael, *Horeb*: *A Philosophy of Jewish Laws and Observances*, translated from the German by I. Grunfeld, (New York: Soncino Press) 1962, 1968, 1972, 1981, pp. 280-281.

Bal Tashchit

Text Study: The Law of *Bal Tashchit*

Participant Worksheet

1) Read Deuteronomy 20:19-20 again. Using *kal v' homer* reasoning, how do you think the Rabbis may have extended this law?

2) What might have been the Rabbis' reason to extend this law?

3) What does a fruit tree symbolize? What is its importance?

4) Jews have invoked the principle of *bal tashchit* in all instances of wanton destruction. It is said that there was a Rabbi who used to cry whenever his students would pick a leaf off of a tree unnecessarily. But what happens when there is a more pressing human need at stake? What if you need to cut down a fruit tree because it is on the site that you have purchased to build a synagogue or a hospital?

5) Can you spray dandelions because you don't like them?

6) Can you weed your garden?

Bal Tashchit

Text Study: The Law of *Bal Tashchit*

Leader Worksheet

1) Read Deuteronomy 20:19-20 again. Using *kal v' homer* reasoning, how do you think the Rabbis may have extended this law?
They extended the prohibition of cutting down trees in time of war (hard situation) to any unnecessary destruction of anything (easier situation). Specifically, the Rabbis said that "Whoever breaks vessels or rips up garments, destroys a building, stops up a fountain, or ruin foods guilty of violating the prohibition of *bal tashchit*."

2) What might have been the Rabbis' reason to extend this law?
If the destruction of fruit trees is prohibited in a time of war, when one would most likely destroy them (we are all familiar with the scorched earth policy of many armies: at wartime, opponents become demoralized through the total destruction of the environment), then it is certainly prohibited to cut fruit trees down in times of peace, when one is not likely to do so.

3) What does a fruit tree symbolize? What is its importance?
To the rabbinic mind, the fruit tree is a gift from God that is useful to humans. It has a purpose: to bear fruit that serves the rest of creation. A fruit tree should be used for the purpose of feeding people and other creatures. To use a fruit tree for any other purpose would be needless waste and destruction. Furthermore, the trees are harmless and vulnerable, and should be allowed to live in most situations.

Jews have invoked the principle of *bal tashchit* in all instances of wanton destruction. It is said that there was a Rabbi who used to cry whenever his students would pick a leaf off of a tree unnecessarily. But what happens when there is a more pressing human need at stake? What if you need to cut down a fruit tree because it is on the site that you have purchased to build a synagogue or a hospital?
Rabbis have often made the choice that is best for the community. If destruction is needed for a higher goal, then it ceases to be destruction; it is then "wise use." The challenge, then, is to determine what is the "common good."

5) Can you spray dandelions because you don't like them?
Not if it is purely for your convenience.

6) Can you weed your garden?
Yes, this insures the greater good of the garden; with fewer weeds, your vegetables will receive ample sunlight and nutrients, and will grow more successfully.

What Do You Know About Waste?

Participant Worksheet

What D'you Know Quiz

1. What percentage of paper used yearly in the United States is used just for packaging?

a. 8%   b. 23%   c. 50%

2. If you are an average adult who weighs 150 pounds, how much garbage will you generate in your lifetime?

a. 1 ton (2,000 lbs.)   b. 10 tons (20,000 lbs.)   c. 45 tons (90,000 lbs.)

3. If all the aluminum thrown away in the U.S. were recycled, how long would it take to gather enough aluminum to rebuild all the commercial airliners in the U.S.?

a. 10 years.   b. 2 years   c. 3 months

4. How much of your garbage is packaging that you throw out immediately?

a.10%   b. 18%   c. 33%

5. The paper equivalent of how many trees is used each week to supply U.S. citizens with the Sunday newspaper?

a. 10,000 trees   b. 50,000 trees   c. 500,000 trees

6. What is the percentage of newspapers that are thrown away and not recycled?

a. 25%   b. 48%   c. 71%

7. Which of the following breaks down first in a landfill?

a. paper cup   b. plastic cup   c. aluminum can   d. none of the above

8. Which country uses half as many resources as we do in the U.S. to produce a single manufactured item?

a. Japan   b. Germany   c. Sweden   d. all of the above

Bal Tashchit

What Do You Know About Waste?

Leader Worksheet

What D'you Know Quiz

1. What percentage of paper used yearly in the United States is used just for packaging?

   a. 8%   b. 23%   c. 50%

2. If you are an average adult who weighs 150 pounds, how much garbage will you generate in your lifetime?

   a. 1 ton (2,000 lbs.)   b. 10 tons (20,000 lbs.)   c. 45 tons (90,000 lbs.)

3. If all the aluminum thrown away in the U.S. were recycled, how long would it take to gather enough aluminum to rebuild all the commercial airliners in the U.S.?

   a. 10 years.   b. 2 years   c. 3 months

4. How much of your garbage is packaging that you throw out immediately?

   a.10%   b. 18%   c. 33%

5. The paper equivalent of how many trees is used each week to supply U.S. citizens with the Sunday newspaper?

   a. 10,000 trees   b. 50,000 trees   c. 500,000 trees

6. What is the percentage of newspapers that are thrown away and not recycled?

   a. 25%   b. 48%   c. 71%

7. Which of the following breaks down first in a landfill?

   a. paper cup   b. plastic cup   c. aluminum can   d. none of the above

8. Which country uses half as many resources as we do in the U.S. to produce a single manufactured item?

   a. Japan   b. Germany   c. Sweden   d. all of the above

Answers: 1. a, 2. c, 3. c, 4. c, 5. c, 6. c, 7 .d (most landfill contents are "mummified" because there is no air to catalyze the breakdown), 8. d

Source of Information: *50 Simple Things you can do to Save the Earth*

Ecology and the environment can not be separated from other societal concerns.

They are intimately related, for the environment is the habitat in which all

societal interactions take place. Therefore, what is done in the name of human

society or social progress will have ramifications for the environment, and what

is done on behalf of the environment will have an effect on our society. In

Judaism, environmental and social concerns are inextricably linked through

tikkun olam, repair of the world. For, in participating in an act of *tikkun olam*,

we step outside ourselves and our own needs and put the needs of others, the

community, and the world first. In a multitude of ways, Judaism helps us get

beyond our self-centeredness and look toward the common good. Taken

together, prayers and holidays, *Torah* study in the broadest sense, and the

practice of *mitzvot* offer a way of life that will insure the common good and the

future of the earth. In this chapter we will look at how Judaism views the links

between environmental concerns and social justice and we will embark on a

tikkun olam project that involves both.

OBJECTIVES

•Participants will discuss the story of the "breaking of the vessels" and the related *mitzvah* (commandment) of *tikkun olam*.
•Participants will describe some of the connections that Jewish texts draw between environmental issues and other social concerns.
•Participants will identify and participate in a *tikkun olam* activity.

MATERIALS & PREPARATION

•A recording of Bob Dylan's song "Everything Is Broken" from his *Oh Mercy* album, and audio equipment.
•Copies of all Readings & Worksheets for participants.
•Have participants bring in newspaper articles that show the connections between environment and other societal issues

OR

•Participants should arrange to have a representative from the organization they have been researching give a five-minute presentation (follow-up from "The Human Place" unit, "Getting Involved" activity).

Ecology, Judaism and *Tikkun Olam*

Opening ▲

Play the song "Everything Is Broken" by Bob Dylan as participants are entering the room; give them copies of the lyrics or write the lyrics on the blackboard. (See Readings & Worksheets)

When the song ends, briefly discuss:

•What is Dylan saying about the state of the world when he declares that "everything is broken"?

•Do you agree with the song's message about the state of our environment ("take a deep breath, feel like you're chokin'—everything is broken")? Do you see the song as an accurate appraisal of other social concerns?

•What is the mood of the song? Does it offer any hope? Do you think there is hope for our broken world?

•Do you think Judaism portrays the world as a broken place?

Repairing the World ▲▲

In "Everything Is Broken," Bob Dylan portrays the world as a shattered place in need of healing. The *Kabbalistic* Jewish tradition also speaks of the shattered nature of our earth. "Repairing the World" (see Readings & Worksheets) is a Jewish story explaining how the world was plunged into this broken state.

Hand out copies of "Repairing the World." Have a volunteer read it to the class, or have the participants take turns reading.

95

DISCUSSION QUESTIONS

•Rabbi Luria's story is a sort of creation myth—a tale that offers insight into why the world works the way it does. What does this story of the breaking of the vessels (sh'virat ha-kaylim) say about evil and suffering in the world?

It implies that although God wished to create a world without pain and suffering, such a world cannot exist unless we help to create it. Evil and great distress arise from the imperfect nature of this world; they have been with us from the beginning.

•Is this myth a hopeful one? Do you think the world is "fixable"?

Unlike Dylan's song, Rabbi Luria's story of our world's brokenness goes on to explain how we can begin to mend the world through tikkun olam *(repair of the world). As bad as things may seem at times, this story insists that there is hope for the future— that through our actions we can repair the creation.*

•One corollary of the story is that everything we do in life matters a great deal. All of our actions move the world a bit, either toward *tikkun* (mending) or further brokenness. Do you agree with this appraisal? What does it tell you about how to live your life?

Many people think their lives make little difference in the grand scheme of things. Luria's story takes issue with this opinion. If you believe that everything you do somehow affects the state of the world, you might pay greater attention to your actions and strive to hasten the tikkun.

•How do you think environmental issues fit into this story and its message of repairing the world?

The story's central metaphor seems to describe the state of our planet's health in a concrete manner. Environmentally speaking, the brokenness of our earth is apparent everywhere—in polluted waters, holes in the ozone layer, global warming, etc. Too often we have been the ones shattering the environment rather than repairing it. We can turn this around and engage in acts of tikkun.

•Our world is broken in many ways. Everywhere you look you see it: poverty, hunger, homelessness, war, disease, racism, sexism, and so many other forms of injustice. Some critics of the environmental movement argue that in the face of such problems, environmental issues should take a back seat. They maintain that we need to repair other, more pressing problems before turning to the state of the natural world. How would you respond to this argument?

These issues do not exist in a vacuum. They are, in fact, all related. By opposing war, for instance, one also stands against the havoc that it wreaks upon the environment. It is also important to emphasize that poor people are disproportionately affected by environmental problems. In the next section of this lesson, we will explore in greater depth the connections that our tradition draws between environmental concerns and other aspects of tikkun olam.

Text Study: Environment and Social Justice ▲▲

Community is the heart of the Jewish way of life. Building a community is not necessarily easy. Living in proximity to people with conflicting needs is difficult, but it can bring great rewards to those who participate in the community building process. The establishment and maintenance of community is a profound strength of Judaism that has enabled our people to survive and flourish throughout history.

Because community is central to the Jewish tradition, environmental concerns are inextricably linked to building community and a better world. In the texts that follow, we will explore the ties between our tradition's environmental awareness and its concern with other matters of *tikkun olam*. Some of the texts will be familiar from previous lessons, but we will be exploring them in a different context.

Four texts are provided. You may divide the group up into 4 sub-groups, giving them time to each focus on one text. Give each participant a copy of the text sheet (see Readings & Worksheets). In the sub-groups, have members read the text aloud and discuss it, drawing parallels between their concern for the environment and the related social issues. For guidance in leading the discussion, consult the Leader Worksheet. After 5-10 minutes, reconvene and have one spokesperson per sub-group present her insights to the larger group.

Getting Involved in *Tikkun Olam* ▲▲

Divide the group into sub-groups of 4 or 5, and give each sub-group a few articles that discuss social justice in the context of environmental work (groups can have the same or different articles). Points to consider: how do these organizations help care for the earth; how do these organizations contribute to society; how do these efforts look toward the future; which organizations would you like to be involved with, or know more about? Have participants discuss with their groups one action each individual can commit to accomplishing within the next seven days.

OR

Follow-up on "Getting Involved" from "The Human Place." If the participants researched environmental organizations, invite representatives from the various groups to speak to the class or have the various groups do extensive presentations about the findings of their research.

• Have a volunteer explain *tikkun olam* to the guests.

• Representatives from the organizations can give five-minute presentations to the class about their work in the region. The three or four guests can then answer questions as a panel.

•Have the participants and guests brainstorm possible actions each individual could take within the next seven days that would move their small corner of the world toward *tikkun olam* (fertilize a sidewalk plant that is looking unhealthy, work in a community garden that donates produce to those in need, work with one of the organizations represented on the panel, etc.). Write these ideas on the board.

•Before they leave, participants can identify one action they will personally take this week, and commit to doing it. Set up a calendarto monitor their follow-through.

Bringing It Home ▲

Cooperation lies at the core of repairing the world and building a good, rich and rewarding life. The community is at the heart of the Jewish tradition; our dedication to the good of the whole and sometimes at the expense of individual parts, is what has kept Judaism alive through the centuries.

To close, have a volunteer read the following story. In the coming week, encourage the group members to be aware of their efforts to cooperate, build community and repair the world.

Someone once inquired what the difference was between heaven and hell, and was first transported to hell. Lo and behold, it was a gorgeous place with green flowing hills, lush valleys and fragrant wildflowers everywhere. Soon the visitor came to a magnificent castle, where outside on the lawn was a banquet table, piled up with the most sumptuous foods imaginable. Many people sat at the table, and they all had huge, four-foot-long forks pegged to their arms. No one could get a morsel of food, for the forks were too long to get to their mouths.

Having seen hell, our visitor was now transported to heaven. Surprisingly enough, it looked exactly the same as hell: the same hills, valleys, flowers, castle, lawn, and even the same amazing banquet table. Here, too, the people at the table had four-foot forks pegged to their arms. But there was one difference. Here, no one was hungry, because the inhabitants of heaven used their long forks to feed their neighbors.

Ecology, Judaism and *Tikkun Olam*:

Opening: Song Lyrics

Reading

Bob Dylan, "Everything Is Broken"

Broken lines, broken strings, broken threads, broken springs
Broken idols, broken heads, people sleeping in broken beds
Ain't no use jivin', ain't no use jokin'—everything is broken.

Broken bottles, broken plates, broken switches, broken gates
Broken dishes, broken parts, streets are filled with broken hearts
Broken words never meant to be spoken—everything is broken.

Seems like every time you stop and turn around
Something else has just hit the ground.

Broken cutters, broken saws, broken buckles, broken laws
Broken bodies, broken bones, broken voices on broken phones
Take a deep breath, feel like you're chokin'—everything is broken.

Every time you leave and go off some place
Things fall to pieces in my face.

Broken hands on broken plows, broken treaties, broken vows
Broken pipes, broken tools, people bendin' broken rules
Hound dog howlin', bull frog croakin'—everything is broken.

Ecology, Judaism and *Tikkun Olam*

"Repairing the World:" From Lawrence Kushner, *The Book of Miracles*, pp. 47-50.

Reading

In sixteenth-century Tsefat, Rabbi Isaac Luria observed that in his world, like ours, many things seemed to be wrong. People suffered from hunger, disease, hatred, and war. "How could God allow such terrible things to happen?" wondered Luria. "Perhaps," he suggested, "it is because God needs our help." He explained his answer with a mystical story.

When first setting out to make the world, God planned to pour a Holy Light into everything in order to make it real. God prepared vessels to contain the Holy Light. But something went wrong. The light was so bright that the vessels burst, shattering into millions of broken pieces like dishes dropped on the floor. The Hebrew phrase which Luria used for this "breaking of the vessels" is *sh'virat ha-kaylim*.

Our world is a mess because it is filled with broken fragments. When people fight and hurt one another, they allow the world to remain shattered. The same can be said of people who have pantries filled with food and let others starve. According to Luria, we live in a cosmic heap of broken pieces, and God cannot repair it alone.

That is why God created us and gave us freedom of choice. We are free to do whatever we please with our world. We can allow things to remain broken or, as Luria urged, we can try to repair the mess. Luria's Hebrew phrase for "repairing the world" is *tikkun olam*.

As Jews, our most important task in life is to find what is broken in our world and repair it. The commandments in the *Torah* instruct us, not only on how to live as Jews, but on how to mend creation.

At the very beginning of the Book of Genesis (2:15) we read that God put Adam and Eve in the Garden of Eden and told them not to eat from the tree of knowledge. God also told them that it was their job to take care of the garden and to protect it.

The stories in the *Torah* tell not only of what happened long ago but also of what happens in each generation. The stories happen over and over again in the life of each person. The Garden of Eden is our world, and we are Adam and Eve. When God says, "Take care of the garden and protect it," God says to us, "Take care of your world and protect it."

According to one *midrash*, God showed Adam and Eve the Garden of Eden and said, "I have made the whole thing for you, so please take good care of it. If you wreck it, there will be no one else to repair it other than you" (Ecclesiastes Rabbah 7:13).

When you see something that is broken, fix it. When you find something that is lost, return it. When you see something that needs to be done, do it. In that way, you will take care of your world and repair creation. If all the people in the world were to do so, our world would truly be a Garden of Eden, the way God meant it to be. If everything broken could be repaired, then everyone and everything would fit together like the pieces of one gigantic jigsaw puzzle. But, for people to begin the great task of repairing creation, they first must take responsibility.

Ecology, Judaism and *Tikkun Olam*

Text Study: Environment and Social Justice: #1: Caring for the Land

Participant Worksheet

As you read your assigned text, ask yourselves: What are the links connecting this text, the environment and social justice? Try to apply the text to societal concerns beyond environment.

Count seven weeks of years [49]. . . . Then blow the horn loudly, on the tenth day of the seventh month —the Day of Atonement—you will sound the horn throughout your land and you will make the fiftieth year holy. You will proclaim release throughout the land for all its inhabitants. It will be a jubilee for you: each of you will return to his holding and each of you will return to his family. That fiftieth year will be a jubilee for you: you will not sow, nor reap the aftergrowth or harvest the untrimmed vines.
—Leviticus 25:8-12

Shabbat and the sabbatical year afford the land the ecologically sound practice of taking a rest. Now we turn to the idea of the jubilee as a time of release of all debts.

1. In ancient Israel, at each jubilee year, land was re-distributed, so that anyone who had accumulated large parcels of land over the past fifty years had to return it to its original "owners" (tenants, actually, since God is the real owner).

Why do you think there was a need for this law?

How might some individuals have accumulated large parcels of land?

What do you think happened to the former "owners" who were "bought out"?

Do you think this was just?

2. How might the principles of this law be applied today?

Ecology, Judaism and *Tikkun Olam*

Text Study: Environment and Social Justice: #1: Caring for the Land

Leader Worksheet

Count seven weeks of years [49]. . . . Then blow the horn loudly, on the tenth day of the seventh month —the Day of Atonement—you will sound the horn throughout your land and you will make the fiftieth year holy. You will proclaim release throughout the land for all its inhabitants. It will be a jubilee for you: each of you will return to his holding and each of you will return to his family. That fiftieth year will be a jubilee for you: you will not sow, nor reap the aftergrowth or harvest the untrimmed vines.
—Leviticus 25:8-12

Shabbat and the sabbatical year afford the land the ecologically sound practice of taking a rest. Now we turn to the idea of the jubilee as a time of release of all debts.

1. In ancient Israel, at each jubilee year, land was re-distributed, so that anyone who had accumulated large parcels of land over the past fifty years had to return it to its original "owners" (tenants, actually, since God is the real owner).

Why do you think there was a need for this law?
To maintain an equitable and just society.

How might some individuals have accumulated large parcels of land?
They could buy out people who had owed them large sums of money.

What do you think happened to the former "owners" who were "bought out"?
They may have become servants or homeless.

Do you think this was just?

2. How might the principles of this law be applied today?
Think about international agribusiness, which accumulates huge lots of land in the Third World, at the expense of peasant farmers.

Ecology, Judaism and *Tikkun Olam*

Text Study: Environment and Social Justice: #2: Restraints on Agriculture

Participant Worksheet

As you read your assigned text, ask yourselves as a group: What are the links connecting this text, the environment and social justice? Try to apply the text to societal concerns beyond environment.

When you reap the harvest of your land, you will not reap all the way to the edges of your field, or gather the gleanings of your harvest. You will not pick up every last grape in your vineyard, or gather the fallen fruit of your vineyard. Leave them for the poor and the stranger: I the Eternal One am your God.
—Leviticus 19:9-10

When you reap the harvest in your field and overlook a sheaf in the field, do not turn back to get it; it will go to the stranger, the orphan and the widow—in order that the Eternal, your God may bless you in all your undertakings.
—Deuteronomy 24:19

Laws concerning the gleanings, the edges of the field, and the forgotten sheaves provide restraints on the agricultural practices of ancient Israelites and some modern Jews. They limit overproduction and remind the farmer that even in a non-sabbatical year, the land cannot be overworked. The laws outline sound ecological practice. Ecology and *tzedakah* (the pursuit of a just society) converge in these laws, for they are also a means of providing for the poor and powerless. As long as people followed these *mitzvot*, no one went hungry.

1. Why do you think the *Torah* prescribed this particular manner for providing for the poor? After all it could have commanded us to support soup kitchens. Do you think this was an effort to explicitly link *tzedakah* and ecology?

2. Is there any current policy that serves to limit overproduction and exhaustion of the soil? Is there a connection between such a policy and feeding the poor?

3. What are some ways that you could practice stewardship and *tzedakah* together in your community?

Ecology, Judaism and *Tikkun Olam*

Text Study: Environment and Social Justice: #2: Restraints on Agriculture

Leader Worksheet

When you reap the harvest of your land, you will not reap all the way to the edges of your field, or gather the gleanings of your harvest. You will not pick up every last grape in your vineyard, or gather the fallen fruit of your vineyard. Leave them for the poor and the stranger: I the Eternal One am your God.
—Leviticus 19:9-10

When you reap the harvest in your field and overlook a sheaf in the field, do not turn back to get it; it will go to the stranger, the orphan and the widow—in order that the Eternal, your God may bless you in all your undertakings.
—Deuteronomy 24:19

Laws concerning the gleanings, the edges of the field, and the forgotten sheaves provide restraints on the agricultural practices of ancient Israelites and some modern Jews. They limit overproduction and remind the farmer that even in a non-sabbatical year, the land cannot be overworked. The laws outline sound ecological practice. Ecology and *tzedakah* (the pursuit of a just society) converge in these laws, for they are, of course, also a means of providing for the poor and powerless. As long as people followed these *mitzvot*, no one went hungry.

1. Why do you think the *Torah* prescribed this particular manner for providing for the poor? After all it could have commanded us to support soup kitchens. Do you think this was an effort to explicitly link *tzedakah* and ecology?
Growing crops, participating in the market, all the activities of life were part of one organic whole; every aspect of life was inextricably linked. Thus this form of tzedakah made organic sense, given the rhythms of time in the ancient world.

2. Is there any current policy that serves to limit overproduction and exhaustion of the soil? Is there a connection between such a policy and feeding the poor?
Such a connection does exist: however, it is a twisted version of the Jewish laws that we have been studying.
Governments today limit production, by telling farmers what to plant and how much. In this case they are regulating supply. They pay farmers not to produce. They limit production to keep demand healthy and prices high. They also regulate demand by buying up the surplus. This surplus often just sits in warehouses. A small amount of it goes to feed the poor, but much of it is wasted. By buying up surplus, the government is keeping supply lower. When supply is lower and the demand remains constant, the prices go up. Creating a higher price is a way for the government to appease the farmers who are not allowed to grow to capacity. If the government gave the surplus away to the poor instead of making them pay, then the demand would decrease (fewer buyers in the market), the supply would remain the same, and the prices would fall. This would displease the farmers.

3. What are some ways that you could practice stewardship and *tzedakah* together in your community?

A few examples: growing a garden and donating the produce. Establishing a food garden at a homeless shelter. Providing employment for the hungry/homeless in conservation activities (building trails, cleaning parks, etc.—a revised version of the Civilian Conservation Corps of the New Deal).

Ecology, Judaism and *Tikkun Olam*

Text Study: Environment and Social Justice: #3: Environmental Legislation

Participant Worksheet

As you read your assigned text, ask yourselves as a group: What are the links connecting this text, the environment and social justice? Try to apply the text to societal concerns beyond environment.

Carcasses, cemeteries and tanneries must be kept at fifty cubits' distance from a town. A tannery can only be set up only on the east side of a town [because the east wind is gentle and will not carry the fumes to town].
—*Mishnah, Baba Batra* 2:9

The connection between this text—legislating the location of cemeteries, tanneries, etc.—and social justice is less obvious than with the previous texts. The link becomes clear only when we consider whom the legislation is designed to protect. Those with sufficient resources can easily choose where they wish to live, thereby avoiding hazards to environmental and physical health. This law acts as a shield for those who lack such resources.

1. Does this law protect a particular social group?

2. Can you think of modern examples of ecological waste sites and hazards that disproportionately affect the poor and lower middle-class?

3. How can we—like the *Mishnah*—expand the blanket of environmental protection so that it covers all members of society, regardless of social class?

4. How do we act as stewards and yet maintain the dignity of those we help?

Ecology, Judaism and *Tikkun Olam*

Text Study: Environment and Social Justice: #3: Environmental Legislation

Leader Worksheet

Carcasses, cemeteries and tanneries must be kept at fifty cubits' distance from a town. A tannery can only be set up only on the east side of a town [because the east wind is gentle and will not carry the fumes to town].
—*Mishnah, Baba Batra* 2:9

The connection between this text—legislating the location of cemeteries, tanneries — and social justice is less obvious than with the previous texts. The link becomes clear only when we consider whom the legislation is designed to protect. Those with sufficient resources can easily choose where they wish to live, thereby avoiding hazards to environmental and physical health. This law acts as a shield for those who lack such resources.

1. Does this law protect a particular social group?
Yes. See above.

2. Can you think of modern examples of ecological waste sites and hazards that disproportionately affect the poor and lower middle-class?
Union Carbide, an American corporation, had a plant in Bhopal, India, which employed thousands of Indians. The Indians provide a source of cheap labor for Union Carbide. A leak in the system at the plant allowed the escape of poisonous gases, and approximately 2000 people in Bhopal were killed. In India, Union Carbide did not use the proper safety precautions that the company would have have had to abide by in the United States.
Mudslides and severe flooding in Bangladesh resulted from the clearcutting of forests. The logging companies profited, while thousands of the area's residents lost their lives.

3. How can we—like the *Mishnah*—expand the blanket of environmental protection so that it covers all members of society, regardless of social class?

4. How do we act as stewards and yet maintain the dignity of those we help?

Ecology, Judaism and *Tikkun Olam*

Text Study: Environment and Social Justice: #4: The Importance of Long-term Thinking

Participant Worksheet

As you read your assigned text, ask yourselves as a group: What are the links connecting this text, the environment and social justice? Try to apply the text to societal concerns beyond environment.

While the sage, Choni, was walking along a road, he saw a man planting a carob tree. Choni asked him: "How long will it take for this tree to bear fruit?"

"Seventy years," replied the man.

Choni then asked: "Are you so healthy a man that you expect to live that length of time and eat its fruit?"

The man answered: "I found a fruitful world because my ancestors planted it for me. Likewise I am planting for my children."
—Babylonian *Talmud, Taanit* 23a.

In this case, too, the connection between environmental thinking and other aspects of *tikkun olam* may not be immediately apparent. The bottom line, however, is that the environmentalists think in terms of the long run, rather than immediate satisfaction.

1. This reading is about the positive effects of long-term thinking. What are some examples of how a lack of long-term thinking hurts both the environment and human beings?

Ecology, Judaism and *Tikkun Olam*

Text Study: Environment and Social Justice: #4: The Importance of Long-term Thinking

Leader Worksheet

While the sage, Choni, was walking along a road, he saw a man planting a carob tree. Choni asked him: "How long will it take for this tree to bear fruit?"

"Seventy years," replied the man.

Choni then asked: "Are you so healthy a man that you expect to live that length of time and eat its fruit?"

The man answered: "I found a fruitful world because my ancestors planted it for me. Likewise I am planting for my children."
—Babylonian *Talmud, Taanit* 23a.

In this case, too, the connection between environmental thinking and other aspects of *tikkun olam* may not be immediately apparent. The bottom line, however, is that the environmentalists think in terms of the long run, rather than in terms of immediate satisfaction.

1. This reading is about the positive effects of long-term thinking. What are some examples of how a lack of long-term thinking hurts both the environment and human beings?
The "development" plans of many governments focus entirely on short-term profits, with little care for what the distant future may bring. Thus, the rain forests are cleared from land that will barely sustain agriculture for five years. A decade later, the soil is eroded; the forests are lost forever, global warming has advanced, and thousands of peasant farmers are left landless, unemployed and hungry.

The first cities began to spring up about 100,000 years ago. City living provided the advantages of security, division of labor and a work force. In modern times, the development of cities has altered the environment considerably. Every year millions of acres of land are covered with cement. High concentrations of people in cities overwhelm natural cleaning systems, creating an enormous amount of waste and pollution. In addition, there are spiritual and psychological ramifications of the ever-increasing urbanization, for those who live in cities become divorced from the natural world.

Judaism has dealt with issues surrounding communities since the beginning of our history. Both the Bible and rabbinic writings recognize the problems that arise when people live in close proximity to each other. To deal with neighborly disputes, the rabbis established laws of neighborly relations codified by Maimonides in his *Hilchot Shechenim* 11:4. In these laws, the good of the community always comes before the good of an individual. Biblical and rabbinic writings have also recognized the need for cities and have created city planning laws that insure the health of the inhabitants, control the growth of cities and improve their livability.

Land use planning and wise urban development is a priority in this age of environmental problems. It is important for citizens to be familiar with the issues and actively participate in the sensible development of their own communities. Community involvement can be empowering as well as creative and fun. The goal of the following exercise is to give participants an opportunity to use what they have learned about traditional Jewish town planning, and engage them in a process of planning an ideal community.

•Participants will identify and discuss some of the land-use policies defined by the Jewish tradition.

•Participants will be encouraged to get involved with land-use issues.

•A roll of butcher paper or sheets of posterboard.
(If you cannot get butcher paper, make a large sheet of paper by cutting open several brown paper bags so that they lie flat. Cut and tape them together, overlapping the edges about one inch. Turn the sheet over for use.)

•Enough markers for all participants.

•Access to a beach site or a sandtray (optional).

•Copies of the land-use planning texts (see Readings & Worksheets).

Design A Community
by Matthew Biers

Opening ▲

Have a volunteer read this passage to the group, but do not reveal its source right away:

> "The quality of urban air compared to the air in the deserts and forests is like thick and turbulent water compared to pure and light water. In the cities with their tall buildings and narrow roads, the pollution that comes from their residents, their waste makes their entire air reeking and thick although no one is aware of it. Because we grow up in cities and become used to them, we can at least choose a city with an open horizon. And if you have no choice, and you cannot move out of the city, try at least to live upwind. Let your house be tall and the court wide enough to permit the northern wind and the sun to come through, because the sun thins out the pollution of the air."

—Moses Maimonides, *The Preservation of Youth: The Guide to Health*, pp.70-71.

DISCUSSION QUESTIONS

•Can you guess when this was written?
Some time between 1190 and 1200 C.E.

•How does this compare to our situation today?

•Do you agree with Maimonides' solutions?
It seems that Maimonides was writing to urge people to protect themselves from urban pollution; he was not addressing the causes of and solutions to the problem. Living upwind of a foul-smelling city may help alleviate or prevent health problems, but it does not stop the pollution.
If those able to move to more desirable locations ("upwind") do so, those left will most likely be without the financial resources to move. This, in fact, is often the case. Poor people are more often affected by pollutants than wealthier people.

Sunlight will make a carbon monoxide haze even worse. This is, of course, not the pollutant that Maimonides mentions. He is correct in his belief that open spaces ("a wide court") with good air circulation can improve the air quality, but today's pollutants are carried so far by winds that they often settle in other countries (for example, acid rain and other airborne pollutants).

How does our modern Ameican society address these problems?
Through local, state and federal legislation and regulations. Zoning boards and town councils administer local land use, such as the proximity of business and residences, the location of the town dump, and parking availability.

Today's Urban Blight ▲

Whether we live in the city, the suburbs or rural areas, we find things that are pleasing to us along with whatever problems we are aware of. Often the problems are socio-environmental, as we discussed in the previous chapter.

As a group, generate a list of socio-environmental problems connected with modern living. (Remember, everything is connected!) Again, let participants be enthusiastic about these problems. This is a good way to release our frustrations about the problems. After we get these off our chests, we can move on to productive solutions.

Text Study: Jewish Land Use ▲

Many Jews, including Maimonides, have tried to improve the quality of urban life by making land-use planning laws. Give each participant a copy of the Jewish land-use text sheet (see Readings & Worksheets). You may use the following questions as a guide for group reading and discussion, and/or ask the participants to keep these in mind while they read to themselves.

•What was the original purpose of the regulations?

•Which considerations do you think are relevant to today's problems?

•In view of contemporary problems, rank the texts from most to least important.

Design a Community ▲▲▲

The group will now have a chance to design a perfect community. Participants will make a map of a town, taking into consideration the laws they have just discussed. First, make a list on the blackboard or on newsprint of all the things the participants want in their community. Some things they will probably want to include are schools, civil services such as police and fire stations, a hospital, provisions for garbage disposal, recycling plants, industry, residences, parks and shops. They may also consider including sources of water and food (reservoirs and farm land).

Have the class gather around the large piece of paper (butcher paper or posterboard). With a pencil, map out the town, taking into consideration the laws you have discussed and participants' own ideas. For example, they may consider having all cars park on the outskirts of town, providing public transportation within the town. They may decide that downtown should be a big park with no cars anywhere, only non-motorized vehicles. Do they want to include bike trails? Where is the industry in relation to the residences? What way do the predominant winds blow? What transportation is available between industry and residential areas? Let them use their imagination. Do they want open-air cafes at every corner so people can gather and enjoy the outdoors and the community? Remember to think about societal concerns as well: making services available to the elderly and providing ramps and sloped curbs for wheelchair access, etc. Debates may spontaneously arise out of this exercise; let the participants struggle with them and try to lead them to a resolution.

If you have access to a beach, or a large sandtray, the participants can build their community in the sand. Have each group member take responsibility for building a different part of the town. If you are staying indoors, have participants decorate the map, using the pencil-drawn guidelines.

Bringing It Home ▲

Land-use policy is usually decided on a local level. An elected city council holds meetings to discuss these issues. Concerned individuals or groups may attend the meetings to voice their opinions and participate in the decision-making process, or they may write letters to the council. Some towns also have a citizens' advisory board, which makes recommendations to the zoning board. Are there relevant issues currently under discussion in your town? Participants may consider attending a meeting or writing a letter concerning a local land-use issue.

Design a Community

Text Study: Jewish Land-Use

Reading

1) You must not raise goats or sheep in the land of Israel because their grazing spoils the land.
—Babylonian *Talmud, Baba Kam*a 79b

(Sheep and goats graze so low to the ground that the plants are unable to regenerate. The plants die and the soil that once bore vegetation, becomes a desert, incapable of putting forth vegetation. This law may be extended to mean that anything that spoils the land should not be grown in Israel.)

2) All cities must have a *migrash* [open space] that surrounds them. The first 1000 cubits [approximately 500 meters] shall be for open space and the next 1000 cubits for grazing animals.
—Numbers 35:2-5 with commentary from Maimonidies.

3) It is forbidden to live in a city that does not have greenery.
—Jerusalem *Talmud, Kiddushin* 12:12

4) Carcasses, cemeteries and tanneries must be kept at fifty cubits' distance from a town. A tannery can only be set up on the east side of a town [because the east wind is gentle and will not carry the fumes to town].
—*Mishnah, Baba Batra* 2:9.

("Carcasses" refers to decaying flesh. In this case it probably refers to a dumpsite. Tanneries were the big industry in rabbinic times; tanning is a process by which a hide is made into leather—it is soaked in tannin which was toxic, this was a very smelly process. This law may be extended to include modern industries that emit a variety of pollutants.)

5) Threshing floors must be 50 cubits outside the city-limits and away from neighbors fields.
—Babylonian *Talmud, Baba Batra* 24b

(A threshing floor was the place where the wheat was beat out of its husk, the chaff. Chaff from a threshing floor can harm people. This law shows that an individual cannot do his own work without thought of the good of the whole community.)

6) The land must not be sold beyond reclaim, for the land is Mine; you are but strangers resident with Me. Throughout the land that you hold, you must provide for its redemption.
—Leviticus 25:23-24

7) [God]... did not create it [the earth] a wasteland, but formed it for habitation.
—Isaiah 45:18

8) The advantage of land is paramount; even the king is subject to the soil.
Ecclesiastes 5:8 (translation: Robert Gordis)

9) Woe to those who add house to house and join field to field, till there is room for no one but you to dwell in the land.
Isaiah 5:8

Time is a chain. We are linked to all those living things that came before us and those which will follow, through a continuous process of creation and evolution.

Time is a circle. Our days are marked by the rotations of the earth, our months by the turning of the moon, and our years by the cycle of earth around the sun.

Jewish prayers and festivals mark the cycles in nature and history. The cycle of the day is acknowledged with prayers at sunrise, mid-day, and sunset; the cycle of the week with *Shabbat*; the cycle of the month with *Rosh Hodesh* (new moon, new month); and the cycles of the seasons with their holiday festivals.

Our lives today are inextricably woven to life in the past, both biologically and historically. We drink the water that our ancestors waded through when they crossed the Red Sea; we look at the same sky that Abraham gazed upon. Those who grasp these links learn awe, humility, and pride. Valuing the past provides a necessary foundation for envisioning the future. The goal of this unit is to demonstrate that both Judaism and ecology place value on the relationships and experiences that occured since the beginnings of time. A second goal is to demonstrate how the Jewish holidays teach us how to live more in tune with nature's rhythms.

•Participants will understand the importance of recalling our ancestors and history and the importance of recognizing our evolutionary relationships with other species—both links to the past.

•Large pieces of cardboard, to make cycle calendars (you can use a large box, broken down).
•Markers or paint and other craft materials
•Copies of Readings & Worksheets for all.

Time

Opening ▲

Have a volunteer read aloud the selections by D.H. Lawrence (see Readings & Worksheets).

Do you feel you are bleeding at the roots? Do you know people who are? Do you agree with Lawrence that our problem today is that we lack a relationship with the natural world and its rhythms? Which Jewish teachings have described a similar problem? Do you believe that ritual can help get us back in touch with nature? What kind of ritual? Does Judaism have rituals that can help us get in touch with natural rhythms? What are they?

POINTS TO EMPHASIZE

Just as no living thing exists independently of its history, the Jewish people are intimately connected to the past.

Jewish tradition grew out of the relationship between a people and their land. Three thousand years ago our ancestors lives revolved around the cycles of the earth. They planted and harvested according to the seasons. They prayed for rain in the winter and dew in the summer. Today our holidays and our lunar calendar are a constant reminder of our interdependence with nature. We honor the new month with *Rosh Hodesh*, blessings of the new moon. We celebrate many holidays on the full moon. We pray in "organic" time at sunrise and sunset.

Connections in Jewish Time ▲

What follows is a series of open-ended questions which address the participants' personal feelings. Of course, most answers are acceptable and should be respected.

•Have you ever wondered why Jewish prayers constantly invoke our ancestors?

•Is it relevant to talk about their experiences? Do you care about what happened to them? What does it have to do with you, anyway?

•How about learning classical Jewish texts? They were written so long ago. Do you think they have value today? Why do you think many people spend their lives studying them?

•What might thse issues have to do with the study of Judaism and ecology?

POINTS TO EMPHASIZE

When Jews pray, we don't just say "Listen to *me*, God." Rather, we say, "*Our* God and God of our *ancestors*," or "God of Abraham, Isaac and Jacob," thereby connecting us to the larger Jewish community and to our ancestors who lived thousands of years ago. Standing here today, we are part of a grand web of life that harkens back to the beginning of time. This web includes all of the natural world: the creatures, lands, waters, and skies which preceded us, as well as all of our human ancestors. This panorama sets the stage for the unfolding of our stories, of our creation today.

We can recall our ancestors, Abraham, Isaac, Jacob, Sarah, Rebecca, Rachel, and Leah, to help give us a sense of place, of belonging. Our ancestors performed truly heroic acts in their daily lives. Knowing their struggles and triumphs can give us a sense of pride and awe. With an involvement in their stories, we have an immediate connection to events that we might otherwise take for granted because they are in the distant past.

Our biological history: the unique adaptations of every creature to its environment like willows to riverside habitats, or monkeys to forests (their tails enable them to swing from tree to tree; we bear witness to our relationship to them with our vestigial tailbone); and our evolutionary and geologic history reflected in places like the Grand Canyon, give a similar sense of awe, humility and pride. An appreciation of the vastness and diversity of life that preceded us is one of the building blocks necessary for molding a sense of stewardship. Respect for the past is a necessary foundation for envisioning the future. We are a link in the chain of life; now it is our turn to see to it that the web is preserved.

Renewing Creation Daily ▲

Recite the prayer *Yotzer Or* (He Who Creates Light) from the daily morning service:

"Praise to You *Adonai*, our God and Universal Ruler. You create light and fashion darkness, and create all. Illuminator of the world and all its creatures with mercy; in Your goodness *You daily renew creation*. How bountiful are Your works, Eternal One, with wisdom You have fashioned them all. The Ruler Who was alone and exalted before creation, Who is praised, glorified, and upraised since the days of old. Eternal

God, with your abundant compassion, be compassionate to us — Master of our power, our rocklike stronghold, shield of our salvation, be a stronghold for us...."

"Through God's Goodness creation is renewed daily. As it is said: [Give thanks] to the One Who makes the great luminaries, for God's kindness endures forever. May You shine a new light on Zion, and may we all merit light speedily. Praise to You, Adonai, Who creates the luminaries."

This prayer tells us that God renews creation daily. What does this mean? Does it mean that every day there is a new sun? When you wake up each Tuesday, the third weekday, are there all new species of plants? On Thursday, the fifth day, new birds? Such notions fly in the face of reason, science and nature. So what is this prayer talking about? How can it be realistically applied to nature? How does it relate to the Jewish perspective on the world?

The Jewish view of creation as an ongoing process rather than a completed act makes evolutionary sense. Some examples of ongoing creation in nature include: rivers cutting deep canyons, volcanoes, islands forming and later disappearing, and the hybridization of plants.

Create A Page of *Talmud* ▲▲▲

Just as creation is a continuous, evolving process, so too are Jewish texts a series of unending commentaries, each building on its predecessors. Ask the participants to give examples. For instance: the Bible has commentary, and the *Haggadah* we read today on Passover is a compilation of many commentaries over the ages (The *Polychrome Haggadah*, provides a wonderful graphic example to illustrate this concept).

The *Talmud* is a testimony to the fact that Jewish tradition has evolved over time. The *Talmud* was an outgrowth of the *Mishnah*, the terse Jewish law code that was compiled in approximately 200 C.E.

The code was so sparse that it was difficult to understand. Over several hundred years, the rabbis struggled with this legacy, writing commentaries of their interpretation of the law. In this way a small bit of *Mishnah* evolved into a full page of *Talmud.* In each generation, Jewish texts are created and renewed, just as God renews the work of creation each day.

Show the group a page of *Talmud* (See Readings & Worksheets). The text is written in Hebrew and Aramaic, a related language of the ancient Middle East. As the participants examine the page, ask them to describe what they see. Even if they cannot read the text, they can point out the different layers and concentric circles of ongoing commentary.

Distribute the "Guide to a Page of *Talmud*" (see Readings & Worksheets). Look at the page of *Talmud,* and consulting the "Guide," emphasize that there are many different sections to a single page of *Talmud*. Again, this is because, unlike most modern works of literature, the *Talmud* was composed by many different sages over a period of centuries.

What to look for:

A. *Mishnah*: the oldest layer, itself made up of many levels. It was compiled by Judah Ha-Nasi around the year 200 C.E. When it appears on a page, it can be found in the middle column of the page in thick Hebrew print.

B. *Gemara*: the next layer, which includes the traditions—often in dispute with one another — of the many Rabbis who commented on the *Mishnah*. It is also in the middle column in Hebrew print like the *Mishnah*.

C. Commentaries: centuries of commentary on the teachings of the *Mishnah* and *Gemara*. Some were written in "Rashi script" (a smaller, rounder typeface) around the edges of the page, framing the *Mishnah* and *Gemara* in the center. The most famous commentaries are those by Rashi (a medieval French commentator) and his disciples and descendants (known as the *Tosafot*). Rashi explained passages of the *Talmud* word for word, commenting on the meaning of each sentence. The *Tosafot,* written much later, raise contradictions within and between different sources.

Participants will now create their own page of "*Talmud*" addressing environmental themes. Divide up into groups of 8-10 participants. Give each group markers and a sheet of posterboard.

Ask the participants to provide the "*Mishnah*" to get things started. They can use any ecological or Jewish principle or law that they have learned in this class to date. Have one participant in each group write it out ("God renews the works of creation daily,"etc.) in the middle of the posterboard. Now have one or two participants in each group offer their own thoughts and comments on that passage. Using a different color marker, they can write their comments in the "*Gemara*" section. When this is done, have another participant respond to the comments now printed in the "*Gemara*." Again, using a different color marker, the participants will write in comments, this time in the "Rashi" section. Continue in this manner until the groups have filled their pages.

The "Sample Page of Student-Created *Talmud*" can serve as a guideline for this activity. Encourage participant commentators to refer to texts and approaches they have studied in previous chapters. When the groups have finished, come back together as a class and read the completed pages. How are they alike? How do they differ? Discuss the process involved. Can the participants who made the earliest comments see how their words served as the seeds for later ideas?

A Jewish Calendar ▲▲▲
by Susan Mack

Using cardboard, paint or markers, and craft materials, the class will make a pie-shaped Jewish calendar. Break the class into small groups and assign each group one piece of the "pie." Each segment of the pie represents a Jewish holiday. The group members should design the section to include the name of the holiday, the corresponding agricultural or seasonal event, and a quote from a Jewish source about that holiday. When all the pieces are completed, reassemble them and glue the full circle to a large piece of cardboard.

If you have enough participants and enough time, create a calendar illustrating the concentric cycles of time acknowledged in Jewish tradition (see sample calendars in Readings & Worksheets section).

Bringing It Home ▲

Think about our spot on the calendar right now. What events in the Jewish cycle are approaching? Making ourselves aware of our place in the Jewish and natural cycle is the *kavannah* for this week.

For Further Reading

Richard Siegel, Michael Strassfeld, and Sharon Strassfeld, *The First Jewish Catalogue*

Arthur Waskow, *Seasons of Our Joy*

Stephen Jay Gould, *Time's Arrow Time's Cycle*

Time

Opening: From D.H. Lawrence

Reading

"A Propos of Lady Chatterly's Lover," *In Phoenix II: Uncollected, Unpublished, and Other Prose Works* by D.H. Lawrence, pp. 504, 510-511

Oh, what a catastrophe, what a maiming of love when it was made a personal, merely personal feeling, taken away from the rising and setting of the sun, and cut off from the magic connection of the solstice and the equinox! This is what is the matter with us, we are bleeding at the roots, because we are cut off from the earth and the sun and stars, and love is a grinning mockery, because poor blossom, we plucked it from its stem on the tree of life, and expected it to keep on blooming in our civilized vase on the table.

It is a question, practically of relationship. We must get back into relation, vivid and nourishing relation to the cosmos. . . The way is through daily ritual, and the reawakening. We must once more practice the ritual of dawn and noon and sunset, the ritual of the kindling fire and pouring water, the ritual of the first breath and the last... We must return to the way of knowing in terms of togetherness. . . the togetherness of the body, the sex, the emotions, the passions, with the earth and sun and stars. The last three thousand years of mankind have been an excursion into ideals, bodilessness, and tragedy and now the excursion is over.

Time

Create a Page of *Talmud*: Guide to a page of *Talmud*

Reading

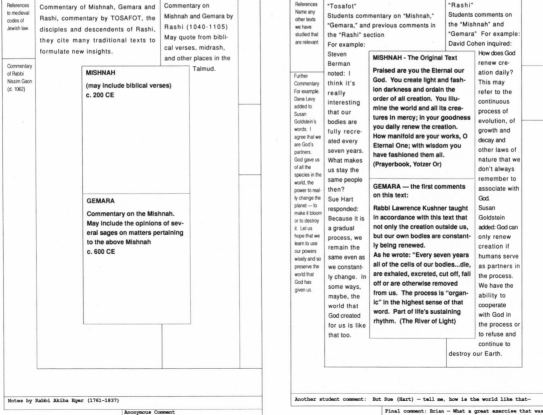

References to medieval codes of Jewish law.	Commentary of Mishnah, Gemara and Rashi, commentary by TOSAFOT, the disciples and descendents of Rashi, they cite many traditional texts to formulate new insights.	Commentary on Mishnah and Gemara by Rashi (1040-1105) May quote from biblical verses, midrash, and other places in the Talmud.

Commentary of Rabbi Nissim Gaon (d. 1062)

MISHNAH

(may include biblical verses)

c. 200 CE

GEMARA

Commentary on the Mishnah. May include the opinions of several sages on matters pertaining to the above Mishnah c. 600 CE

Notes by Rabbi Akiba Eger (1761-1837)

Anonymous Comment

References Name any other texts we have studied that are relevant	"Tosafot" Students commentary on "Mishnah," "Gemara," and previous comments in the "Rashi" section For example: Steven Berman noted: I think it's really interesting that our bodies are fully recreated every seven years. What makes us stay the same people then? Sue Hart responded: Because it is a gradual process, we remain the same even as we constantly change. In some ways, maybe, the world that God created for us is like that too.	"Rashi" Students comments on the "Mishnah" and "Gemara" For example: David Cohen inquired:

Further Commentary For example: Dana Levy added to Susan Goldstein's words: I agree that we are God's partners. God gave us all of the species in the world, the power to really change the planet — to make it bloom or to destroy it. Let us hope that we learn to use our powers wisely and so preserve the world that God has given us.

MISHNAH - The Original Text

Praised are you the Eternal our God. You create light and fashion darkness and ordain the order of all creation. You illumine the world and all its creatures in mercy; in your goodness you daily renew the creation. How manifold are your works, O Eternal One; with wisdom you have fashioned them all. (Prayerbook, Yotzer Or)

GEMARA — the first comments on this text:

Rabbi Lawrence Kushner taught in accordance with this text that not only the creation outside us, but our own bodies are constantly being renewed. As he wrote: "Every seven years all of the cells of our bodies...die, are exhaled, excreted, cut off, fall off or are otherwise removed from us. The process is "organic" in the highest sense of that word. Part of life's sustaining rhythm. (The River of Light)

How does God renew creation daily? This may refer to the continuous process of evolution, of growth and decay and other laws of nature that we don't always remember to associate with God. Susan Goldstein added: God can only renew creation if humans serve as partners in the process. We have the ability to cooperate with God in the process or to refuse and continue to destroy our Earth.

Another student comment: But Sue (Hart) — tell me, how is the world like that—

Final comment: Brian — What a great exercise that was

Create a Page of *Talmud*

Participant Worksheet

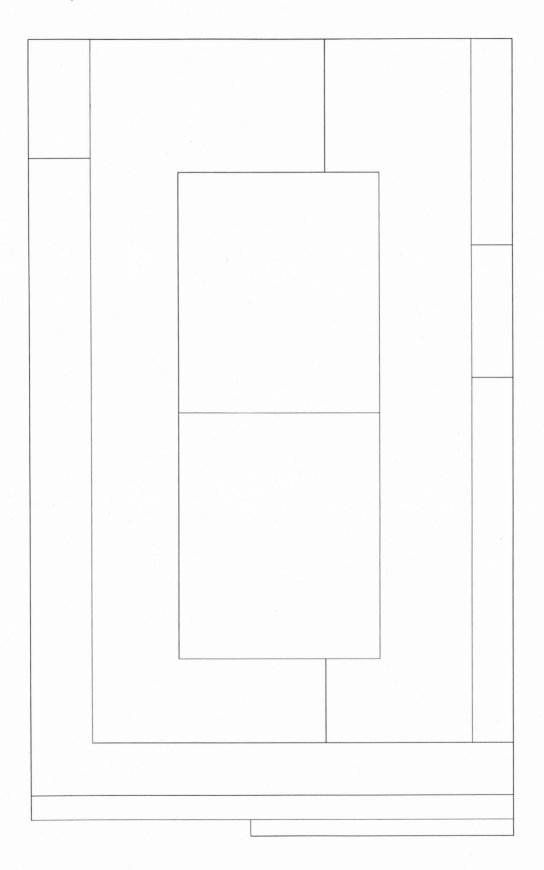

HOW TO MAKE A CIRCULAR CALENDAR

Tools: a compass, a protractor, and a ruler or straight edge.

1. Draw a circle using the compass.

2. Divide 360 by the number of segments you need. If, for instance, you want to illustrate the months of the year, you will need twelve segments.

$$360 \div 12 = 30$$

3. Using the protractor, mark off segments 30 degrees apart. Your marks will be at 30, 60, 90, 120, 150, 180, 210, 240, 270, 300 and 360 degrees. See figure A.

4. Using a ruler or straight edge, draw a line from the center of the circle to each of the marks you have made. See figure B. In the case of concentric circles, line up your ruler the same way, but be sure to draw the line only within the circle you are working on. See figure C.

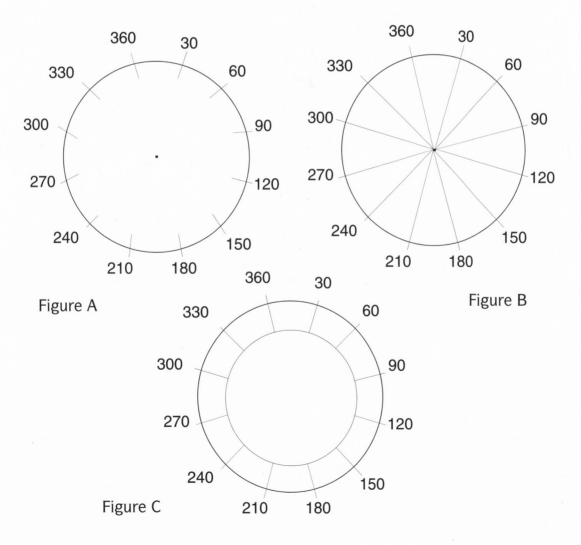

Figure A

Figure B

Figure C

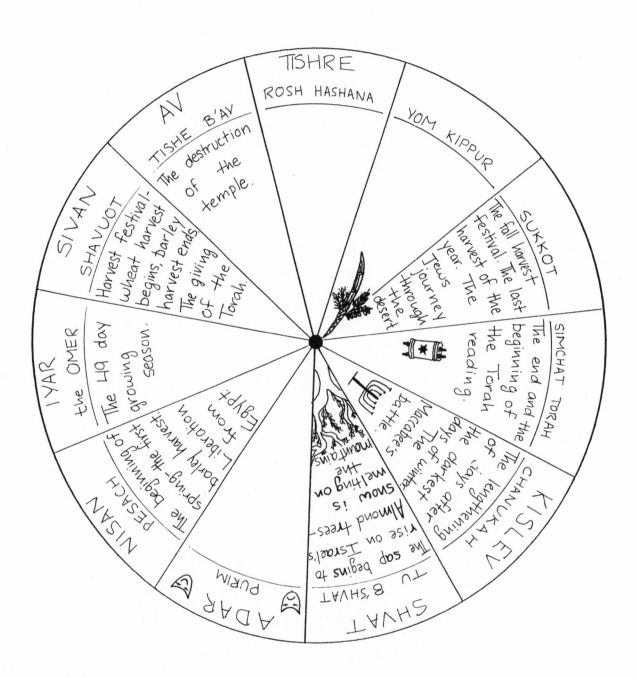

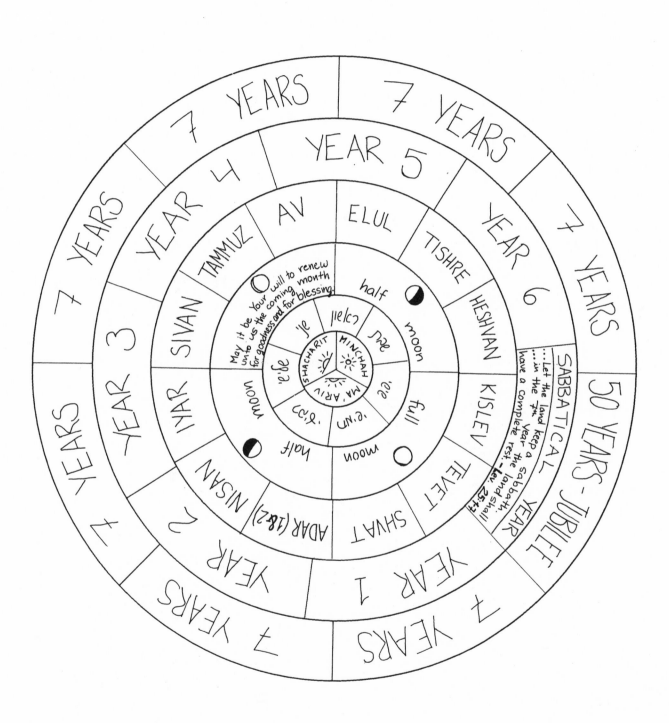

The following suggestions for texts and graphics concentrate on the natural and agricultural aspects of each holiday.

THE YEAR-LONG CYCLE

•Days of Awe

From *Rosh Hashanah* to *Yom Kippur*

Literally, *Rosh Hashanah* means "the head of the year." It is thought that the world was conceived on *Rosh Hashanah* and is judged on *Yom Kippur*.

Text: Today the world was conceived, today they [all creation] will stand in judgement.

—Traditional High Holiday prayer

•*Sukkot*

Sukkot is the autumn harvest festival, marking the final harvest of the year.

Text: On the first day, take the fruit of citron trees, branches of palm, terebinth and willow and celebrate facing God for seven days.

—Leviticus 23:40

•*Channukah*

Channukah marks the longest night of the year. The days begin to lengthen after the winter darkness.

Text: Adam exclaimed when he saw the days getting shorter [in the winter]: "Oh, no! Maybe the world is getting darker because I have sinned!"... But when he saw the days begin to lengthen after the winter solstice, Adam said: "This is the way of the world." So he started observing an eighth day holiday [at this point in time].

—Babylonian *Talmud*, *Avodah Zara* 8a.

•*Tu B'Shvat* (New Year of the Trees)

The ground begins to thaw, the sap begins to rise in Israel's earliest bloomers, the almond tree.

Text: God said, "The land will grow greenery- the kind with seeds on the outside [to be blown about by the wind] and the kind with its seeds on the inside — like the fruit of specific kinds of fruit trees"; and so it was. The land grew greenery... God saw that it was good.

—Genesis 1:11-12

•*Purim*

Like Mardi Gras and Carnival, *Purim* is an early springtime revelry. It is a time to celebrate, visit your neighbors, and share gifts.

Text: Be Happy, it's Adar!
—Traditonal greeting for *Purim* and the whole month around it.

•*Pesach* (Passover)

Pesach is the spring festival. Lambing begins, the cows begin to calve, the first barley is cut. In earlier times, old stores of grain were cleared out to make room for the upcoming harvest, much as we clean our houses of *hametz* (leavened foods) today.

Text: Make a holiday for Me three times a year...eat *matzot* for a spring festival.

—Exodus 23:14

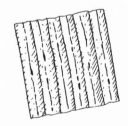

•The *Omer*

The Counting of the *Omer* marks the 49-day growing season, culminating with *Shavuot* on the 50th day. The *Omer* is traditionally an apprehensive time, as farmers watch the progress of their crops, on which their sustenance for the year depends.

Text: Praise to you *Adonai,* our God and universal Ruler, Who makes us holy with Your commandments and commands us to count the *Omer.*

—Prayer for the ritual counting of the *Omer.*

•*Shavuot* (Feast of Weeks)

A harvest festival marking the season's last barley harvest and first wheat harvest. During the time of the Temple, pilgrims came form far and wide to offer *bikkurim* (first fruits) including wheat, barley, grapes, figs, pomegranates, olives and dates. In gratitude for God's gifts, the priests made an offering of two loaves of bread.

Text: Count from the time you bring the *omer*/grain measure...count 50 days and make a grain offering to God...bring two baked breads...made from...the finest flour...first fruits to God...they will make a sweet smell for God...for a peace offer...they will be holy to God...Call it a holiday; do not do any work anywhere.

—Leviticus 23:15-21

•*Tisha B'Av* (the Ninth of Av)

The solemn day marks the destruction of the Temple, the heart of Jewish life in ancient times.

Text: Barley planted, barley sown, barley taken root in the soil, when He blows on them and they dry up and the windstorm lifts them like straw.

—Isaiah 40:24

More Jewish Cycles

•*Shacharit, Minchah,* and *Ma'ariv*

These are the names of the morning, afternoon, and evening prayer services, respectively.

Text: The sun sets and rises, and hastens towards its place.

—Ecclesiastes 1:5

•*Shabbat*

On the seventh day, God rested from creation. Every seventh day, humans rest from creating as well.

Text: The seventh day will be *Shabbat* for God. Do not do any work, [not] you, [not] your son, daughter, male and female slaves, ox, donkey and all your domestic animals [nor] the stranger at your gate. [This is] so your male and female slaves can rest like you.

—Deuteronomy 5:14

•*Rosh Hodesh*

Rosh Hodesh is the new moon and the first day of a new month.

Text: Praise to you ,*Adonai,* our God, Universal Ruer, who created the skies with a word and the stars with a breath. You set for them a law and a time within which to operate. They gladly obey the Creator's will. As the Maker is Truth, so

is the Maker's work Faithfulness. God ordered the moon to renew itself each month- a glorious shining crown- to symbolize Hope to burdened people that they too will be renewed- announcing their Creator's glorious domain. You are Praised, Universal Ruler, who makes the months new.

—Blessing for the the new moon, said outside where you can see the moon.

•*She'vee'it* (Sabbatical Year)

Every seventh year, farmers are to let the land rest from cultivation. This provides a necessary rest for the soil, giving it time replenish itself.

Text: The land will rest — a *Shabbat* for God. You will sow your fields and prune your vineyards, gathering in [the earth's] produce, for six years. The land will have a Sabbath of Sabbaths for God in the seventh year. Do not plant in your fields and do not prune your vineyards.

—Leviticus 25:2-4

•*Yovel,* Jubilee Year

The *Torah* commands us to hold a celebration every 50 years. At this time, the land is released from ownership, all debts are forgiven, and indebted servants go free. The land again lies fallow for any and all to reap.

Text: The land may not be sold forever for it belongs to Me- because you are strangers and temporary residents with Me. [This must be done with] all your land holdings; you will give redemption to the land.

—Leviticus 25: 23-24

We order our days and months and years by the rotations of the earth, the turning of the moon, and the circling of the earth around the sun. Yet one measure of time delineated by our calendars seems completely arbitrary, totally unrelated to any external events or natural phenomemena: the week. Why do we group together periods of seven days? Wouldn't a five or ten day week make at least as much sense?

In fact the week is not arbitrary at all. Our notion of the seven-day week is rooted in the biblical creation story. Ineluctably tied to that story, the Jewish people began to mark time in weeks to celebrate and honor the seventh day as a day of rest. God gave us the *Shabbat* (the Sabbath) and the seven day week came into being.

Shabbat is a weekly reminder that the universe and everything in it belong to God. We are encouraged to remember our place in the divine scheme. By not working and by adhering to the laws of *Shabbat*, we are trained to honor God's creation. For some of us, keeping *Shabbat* may feel binding: too many preparations, too many "don'ts", too many restrictions. But it is possible to view *Shabbat* and its boundaries or limits in another light.

Boundaries and rules give definition. The clear delineation between *Shabbat* and the rest of the week invites us to see the world from a special perspective. *Shabbat* offers us a regular sanctuary of time to let go of our worries, our worldly problems and cares. On *Shabbat* we remember that God is in charge. Knowing that we are not responsible for all of creation gives us a taste of freedom.

The goals of this chapter are to see *Shabbat*, the *she'vee'it* (sabbatical year) and the Jubilee as a pause in the cycle of human-dominated time, and to understand the significance of the these special times as paradigms for the proper use of land and other environmental resources.

OBJECTIVES

•Participants will recognize the temporal dimension of the environmental crisis.
•Participants will know there are prohibitions to working on *Shabbat* and will understand their significance relative to our relation with the environment.

OBJECTIVES

•Participants will recognize the temporal dimension of the environmental crisis.
•Participants will know there are prohibitions to working on *Shabbat* and will understand their significance relative to our relation with the environment.

Shabbat—A Pause in the Cycles

Opening Reading ▲

Have a volunteer read aloud the excerpt from a piece that Jeremy Rifkin wrote for the *Whole Earth Review* (see Readings & Worksheets). He has been an outspoken environmental advocate for many years, and has authored several books.

DISCUSSION QUESTIONS

•Give some examples of how "bigger-is-better" is a predominant spatial value in our society.
We aspire towards bigger homes, more money, more clothes, bigger buildings, more stores, a greater selection of merchandise.

•Give some examples of how "faster-is-better" is a predominant time value in our society.
We aspire towards greater efficiency. We sacrifice quality for quantity. We rush to get as much done in as little time as possible to give us more time to relax. Americans live to work; rather we should strive to work to live.

•Give examples of how our civilization has come to exploit time.
We have reduced nature's cycles to the neat grids of months and dates of our calendar. In doing so, we act as if time and space belong to us to use in the fulfillment of our desires. We learn 3000 years of history in one year. We separate our learning years (childhood and teens) from our work years (adult).

•What's wrong with going too fast? How might it account for environmental problems?
When we are constantly moving and working and trying to achieve new goals, we overlook the gifts of creation. We become obsessed with ourselves as masters. We exploit more and more natural resources in less and less time.

•Can you think of any ways that Judaism offers an antidote to this most insidious environmental problem?

It is incumbent on every generation of Jews to find meaning in the tradition. Today we are confronted with life threatening environmental problems. We can look into our holidays and other aspects of our tradition to glean what it has to teach about ecological concerns. The holidays, Shabbat and the sabbatical year provide a stop-gap measure to the problem of living in the fast lane.

There is a time to plant after Pesach, *a time to count the* Omer, *a time to reap at* Shavuot *and* Sukkot, *a time to be joyful at* Purim, *a time for inner reflection and re-alignment at* Rosh Hashanah *and* Yom Kippur, *time for renewal at each* Rosh Hodesh. Shabbat *offers a weekly release, a letting go from the matters of the world, for humans and nature alike, and the sabbatical year and Jubilee expand on this practice.*

Last in Creation; First in Intention ▲

•How might we restore our time orientation to a healthy balance?

Many environmentalists have advocated a kind of "environmental sabbath". They recommend reserving one day a week to "do" nothing and "use" nothing: no driving (uses precious fuel), no lights or appliances (uses precious resources to make electricity). Rather, they suggest, we should just "be": appreciate creation; stop, slow down, remember our purpose and place; realign ourselves to the deeper meaning in our lives.

They believe that only by taking a total and complete break from our work-a-day world will we attain true self consciousness. It is just too easy to forget; to become oblivious to creation and even to our selves when we are constantly active. We hope that by taking one day of rest, regeneration and renewal each week we can see life and our own lives with a fresh perspective. The rest day can encourage a healthy relationship with the world during the six other work days.

•What value does the Jewish tradition place on its *Shabbat*?

Unlike all other Jewish holidays, Shabbat *precedes the existence of the Jewish people.* Shabbat *is part of the very fabric of creation. It is, by its very nature, a reminder that there are strict limits to human dominion over the natural world.*

According to Jewish tradition, the week exists for the Shabbat. *In the Hebrew, we count all other days with reference to it. Sunday is* Yom Rishon l'Shabbat—*Day One to the Sabbath. Monday is Day Two to the Sabbath and so on. Like a weekly countdown. Only the seventh day has a name:* Shabbat.

As the words of L'chah Dodi *tell us,* Shabbat *is the last in creation- it was created last; however, it is the first in intention; it gives meaning to the rest of creation.*

•How does the environmental sabbath remind you of the Jewish *Shabbat*?
Resting, cultivating appreciation of nature, not driving (for some), "not doing", and spending time with community and friends are all central to both observances.

•What types of work are prohibited on *Shabbat*? Is mowing the lawn work? Driving a car? Shopping? How do you think refraining from such work on *Shabbat* might affect our relationship with the natural world?
According to Jewish tradition, all of the aforementioned activities are prohibited on Shabbat. *This is because our tradition defines "work" as any of 39 activities involved in the building of the sanctuary that the ancient Israelites carried with them through the desert. These actions include: lighting fire, picking up sticks and stones, cutting materials, chopping wood, etc. And while there weren't things like lawnmowers or cars at that time (more than 3000 years ago) the 39 principles have been expanded to encompass these modern activities.*
What is important is the link between "work" and the tasks involved in creating the sanctuary. The texts seem to say that while it is a good thing for humans to use their minds and bodies to create things during the week, on Shabbat *we should refrain from our own creating (work) and instead focus our energies on giving thanks for what God has created.*
This has significant implications for environmentalists. By observing Shabbat, *we remind ourselves that our own technology must not go unchecked or run rough-shod over the beautiful world which God has created and set in our hands.*

•In what ways are do some people's observance of *Shabbat* contradict environmental principles? What could you do to make your *Shabbat* more ecologically sound?
Some families leave lights and ovens on all day and night; this is extremely wasteful and with devices like electric timers, crockpots and hotplates some of the waste can be eliminated while still abiding by the strictures. At synagogue Shabbat *celebrations, paper and plasticware is commonly used and often not recycled.*

•Imagine an entire civilization which does not observe a day of rest. What would be the consequences? What happens to the world; what happens to you? Do you observe Shabbat or do you take one day off a week? Does taking a rest change your perspective on your own life?

POINT TO CONSIDER

Our sages declared that *Shabbat* was a foretaste of the world to come, a harbinger of a day that would be "all *Shabbat*". But they also believed that together with God, we could hasten the arrival of that time. They observed that if all Israel were to keep one (the same) *Shabbat*, the *Mashiach* (messiah) would come (Exodus *Rabbah* 12:5).

Text Study: *Shabbat* and the Sabbatical Year ▲▲▲

Divide the group into pairs, and give each pair a copy of the texts and study questions (see Readings and Worksheets). Regroup after 15 minutes for a discussion of the texts. Use the Leader Worksheet as a guide.

As you read the texts, you will see that we are speaking not only about the ordinary *Shabbat* which occurs each week, but also a sabbatical (*She'vee'it*) year which occurs every seven years. It, too, has great significance as an environmental paradigm.

POINTS TO EMPHASIZE

By encouraging us to rest, *Shabbat* has the potential to free us from the often exploitative work day world, and offers us a vision of a world in which we live in harmony with nature and each other.

Likewise, *She'vee'it,* the sabbatical year and *Yovel,* the jubilee year, remind us that the earth belongs to God. We are tenants here and we are obligated to treat God's creation with respect and care.

Bringing It Home ▲

As we have learned, our tradition mandates a sabbatical year every seventh year and a jubilee every fiftieth year. In the sabbatical year, the land lies fallow. Imagine how the world and particularly the environment would be different if we paid attention to the sabbatical year. How would the world look? Follow your imagination. Be specific. List all the participants' ideas on the blackboard.

For Further Reading

Abraham Joshua Heschel, *The Sabbath: Its Meaning for Modern Man.*

Shabbat: A Pause in the Cycles
Opening: Jeremy Rifkin, *Whole Earth Review*, p. 106
Reading

If "bigger is better" was the primary spacial value of our industrial society, then "faster is better," hyperefficiency, expediency, are the primary temporal values in our worldview. I suggest our time values are the last unchallenged part of our traditional worldview. We need to develop what I would call "slow is beautiful." A sustainable time orientation would be one in which we learned to produce and consume at the rate that nature can recycle and replenish. We need to develop a time orientation that's compatible with the biological frequencies of the planet. While our "computer nanosecond culture" creates a context for more hyperefficiency, the tradeoff and tragedy is that we're becoming a society that feels we have less and less time than any culture on the planet. Yet the average medieval serf had 115 days off a year.

Shabbat: A Pause in the Cycles

Text Study: *Shabbat* and the Sabbatical Year

Readings

1) Remember the Sabbath day and keep it holy. Work for six days but the seventh day is a sabbath of the Lord your God: do not do any work—you, your son or daughter, your male or female servant, or your cattle, or the stranger who is within your gates. For in six days the Lord made the heaven and earth and sea, and all that is in them, and God rested on the seventh day; therefore the Lord blessed the Sabbath day and made it holy.
—Exodus 20:8-11

2) When you come unto the Land which I have given you, then the Land will keep a sabbath for the Lord. For six years sow your field, and for six years prune your vineyard, and gather its produce. But in the seventh year there will be a sabbath for the Lord; neither sow your field nor prune your vineyard. What grows by itself do not reap, and the grapes of your untrimmed vine do not gather; it will be a year of complete rest for the land.
—Leviticus 25:2-5

3) Count off seven weeks of years—seven times seven—so that the period of seven weeks of years gives a total of forty-nine. Then blow the horn loudly; in the seventh month on the tenth day—the Day of Atonement—have the horn sounded throughout your land for all its inhabitants. It will be a jubilee for you. You will proclaim release throughout the land for all its inhabitants. It will be a jubilee for you: each will return to his holding and each will return to his family. . . Do not sow, neither reap the aftergrowth or harvest the untrimmed vines, for it is a jubilee. It will be holy to you: eat only the growth direct from the field. . . And the land will not be sold forever, for the land is Mine; you are but strangers and settlers with me.
—Leviticus 25: 8-12, 23

4) They [the categories of "work" prohibited on *Shabbat*] correspond to the forms of labor in the building of the tabernacle. They [the builders of the tabernacle] sowed, therefore you must not sow [on *Shabbat*]; they reaped, therefore you must not reap; they lifted up boards from the ground to the wagon, therefore you must not carry from a public to a private domain.
—Babylonian *Talmud, Shabbat* 49b

5) ...[T]he Sabbath is a day of harmony and peace, peace between man and man, peace within man, and peace with all things. On the seventh day man has no right to tamper with God's world, to change the state of physical things. It is a day of rest for man and animal alike.
—Abraham Joshua Heschel, *The Sabbath*, p. 31.

6) As a result of the mechanization and overindustrialization of present day life, the human being has come to stand in greater need of the Sabbath than before...The function of the Sabbath is to prohibit man from engaging in work in any way that alters the environment, so that he should not delude himself into the belief that he is complete master of his destiny.
—Rabbi Mordechai Kaplan, *Judaism as a Civilization*, pp. 443-444.

Shabbat: A Pause in the Cycles

Text Study: *Shabbat* and the Sabbatical Year

Participant Worksheet

1. In the verses taken from the Exodus version of the Ten Commandments, God commands us to refrain from working on *Shabbat*. What reason does God give for this prohibition? Why do you think that this *mitzvah*—unlike many others—applies to non-Jews (the stranger among you) and animals as well as the Jewish community? What value do you see in taking one complete day of rest each week?

2. The passages from Leviticus speak of the sabbatical year. They teach us that just as people and animals get a day of rest each week, the land gets a one-year rest period every seven years—a *shabbat* for the land. Why do you think that God commands us to observe this year-long *shabbat* for the land every seven years? Is this sound agricultural and environmental policy? Would it be feasible to observe today?

3. The Leviticus passage also speaks of the jubilee year—a sabbatical of sabbatical years—which occurs after the passage of seven periods of seven years [i.e. after every 49 years, the fiftieth year is the Jubilee]. During that year, all land-holdings were redistributed so that no one could amass too much land on a permanent basis. Do you think that this is fair to landholders? How is this policy related to God's statement that "the land is Mine"? What are the ramifications of this statement for those concerned with environmental issues?

4. The modern Jewish thinker Abraham Joshua Heschel expresses his hope for *Shabbat* as an institution capable of changing the world. What does he see as the source of the Sabbath day's great power? Do you agree with Heschel's belief that by changing the way we relate to each other and to the natural world on one day each week, *Shabbat* observance can lead us to act more responsibly on the other six days?

5. Think of some environmentally-harmful activities which you do during the week and which you might begin to refrain from doing on *Shabbat*. Next *Shabbat*, try giving up one or two of these activities for the day.

Shabbat: A Pause in the Cycles

Text Study: *Shabbat* and the Sabbatical Year

Leader Worksheet

1. In the verses taken from the Exodus version of the Ten Commandments, God commands us to refrain from working on *Shabbat.* What reason is given for this prohibition? Why do you think that this *mitzvah*—unlike many others—applies to non-Jews (the stranger among you) and animals as well as the Jewish community? What value do you see in taking one complete day of rest each week?

The basis for the prohibition against work on Shabbat *is the notion that God rested on that day after God created the world. Creation was the most universal of experiences, an event with deep meaning for all—Jew and Gentile, master and servant, people and other animals. God seems to be teaching by example here—if even God rests once a week, then surely all of God's creatures should do likewise. One value of resting one day each week is to turn our attention from the matters of the world and work to remember who we are, our purpose and place, and celebrate God's creation.*

2. The passages from Leviticus speak of the sabbatical year. They teach us that just as people and animals get a day of rest each week, the land gets a one-year rest period every seven years—a *shabbat* for the land. Why do you think that God commands us to observe this year-long *shabbat* for the land every seven years? Is this sound agricultural and environmental policy? Would it be feasible to observe today?

The sabbatical year may have served several purposes. Like the Shabbat *day, it served to remind human beings that God—not us—is the true Ruler and Creator of our world. But the sabbatical year also reflects wise agricultural/environmental policy. In biblical days, as in our own, people did not understand the needs of the land. They did not intuitively know that the land would wear out (loss of valuable nutrients, erosion) when subjected to continuous planting; they had to learn this. The policy of the sabbatical year for the land was a sound ecological practice which would sustain the land and soils for the future generations.*

Some religious farmers/kibbutzim in Israel do observe the sabbatical year today. Many other farmers observe the spirit of this mitzvah *by properly rotating their crops, composting, and using other methods to keep the earth healthy.*

3. The Leviticus passage also speaks of the jubilee year—a sabbatical of sabbatical years—which occurs after the passage of seven periods of seven years [i.e. after every 49 years, the fiftieth year is the Jubilee]. During that year, all land-holdings were redistributed so that no one could amass too much land on a permanent basis. Do you think that this is fair to landholders? How is this policy related to God's statement that "the land is Mine"? What are the ramifications of this statement for those concerned with environmental issues?

The jubilee year reflects the same attitude that is evident in the psalmist's statement that "the earth is the Eternal One's." If this is the case, it is certainly proper to equitably redistribute land during the Jubilee, since no human being ever really owns it to begin with. We merely work the land, receiving it on loan from God, who continues to affirm that "It is Mine." Most environmentalists would likely approve of such a view; after all, if we are tenants on the land rather than its owners, we have a powerful obligation to treat the land with respect—especially when we acknowledge that God is the landlord!

4. The modern Jewish thinker Abraham Joshua Heschel expresses his hope for *Shabbat* as an institution capable of changing the world. What does he see as the source of the Sabbath day's great power? Do you agree with Heschel's belief that by changing the way we relate to each other and to the natural world on one day each week, *Shabbat* observance can lead us to act more responsibly on the other six days?

Heschel maintains that by refraining from "work" on the Sabbath— thereby detaching ourselves from the everyday world of money, greed, consumption and exploitative technology—we get a small taste of what it would be like to live in a better world. He seems to hope that this "taste" will motivate us to work for such a world—a world where it is, so to speak, Shabbat *every day.* Shabbat *encourages us to strive for the time when all will live in harmony with each other and their environment.*

5. Think of some environmentally-harmful activities which you do during the week and which you might begin to refrain from doing on *Shabbat*. Next *Shabbat*, try giving up one or two of these activities for the day.

Examples might include driving, taking excessively long showers, using paper plates and cups, using electric gadgets, littering, etc.

This lesson provides an opportunity to apply the Jewish environmental

principles we have learned to a real-life situation. Group members participate in

a role-playing exercise in which they debate the pros and cons of logging the

rainforests of South America. The goal of this exercise is to apply Jewish values

in decision-making, while raising awareness of the environmental issues

surrounding rainforest deforestation.

OBJECTIVES

•Participants will use Jewish source material to understand and defend particular positions on environmental questions.

•Participants will discuss some of the issues surrounding continuing rainforest deforestation.

MATERIALS & PREPARATION

•You may want to hand out character profiles to the participants in the meeting prior to this one. Let them know they will be playing this character in a debate on the rainforest. They should come to the meeting prepared to defend their positions. They should review what they have learned about Jewish perspectives on the human relationship with nature in order to fortify their characters' arguments. See "Group Organization" below.

•Copies of the "Opening Address" for all.

•Copies of Character-role sheets for each participant, with group letter assignments.

•Character Development Worksheets for all.

•Blank Sub-Committee Reports (1/ group).

•A map of the Brazilian rainforest.

A Rainforest Roleplay

Opening

Without preamble, deliver an "Opening Address." Use the "transcript" directly (see Readings & Worksheets) or adapt it for your needs. This speech will set the stage for the activity to follow. Deliver the address in character, as though you were a United Nations official giving a sub-committee its mandate.

THE SYMPOSIUM
Group Organization

Assign each participant the role of a Jewish world leader (you may want to do this in the prior meeting). There are 8 different characters. You will be dividing the large group up into sub-committees. Each committee will include each of the 8 characters. This may best be accomplished by assigning a committee letter (A,B,C) to the character worksheets.

If participants disagree with the view of the character they are assigned, the role-play will give them a chance to learn about another viewpoint. Representing characters they disagree with will also help participants guess what the other side will say against their character's viewpoint.

Hand out the following materials:

1) Copies of the Opening Address

2) Role-sheets

3) Character Development Worksheets

Character Preparation ▲

Have the participants complete the Character Development Worksheet. This will help them prepare their statements for their committee's discussion.

Committee Meetings and Reports ▲▲

Divide the characters up into the appropriate groups and assign each group its own space in the room. Each committee's job is to develop a recommendation to the United Nations.

Give one member of each committee a copy of the "Report Recommendation" form. Each committee's task is to complete the report, using Jewish texts to defend its recommendation.

Have each member of the committee deliver a brief opening statement about his/her position, using the worksheet s/he just completed. The members of each committee will discuss and debate until they agree on a recommendation to write down. Remind participants that they have only 20 minutes to create their report. They may want to designate one person in the group to act as time-keeper or facilitator in order to keep things organized. Give a five minute warning. When the time is up, ask someone from each sub-committee to read the group's recommendation aloud.

Conclusion ▲

What made it difficult for your group to reach an agreement for your report? How did your group overcome those difficulties? If your personal opinion was different from your character's view, what was it like to argue your character's position? Was it easy or difficult? Why? What character did you agree with most? What character did you disagree with most?

All of the quotes we used came from Jewish tradition, but they didn't all lead to the same conclusion. How would you decide which Jewish point of view to follow in forming your own opinions? Do you think it's good or bad that the Jewish religion offers many different views? Would it be better or worse if there were only one Jewish viewpoint?

We have found out that even within the Jewish religion, there are different views about what's right and wrong. Jews, including each one of us, can use Jewish texts and the great books of our tradition to help us clarify our beliefs. That is why it is so important to continue studying and learning from these books.

A Rainforest Roleplay

Official Transcript of Opening Statement

Reading

UNITED NATIONS RAINFOREST SYMPOSIUM   February 30, 2001

Delivered by: Chairperson, United Nations Environmental Task Force

As Chairperson of the United Nations Environmental Task Force, I want to welcome you to our Rainforest Symposium. As you know, this conference was called because of world-wide concern over the rapid clearing of rain forest land, particularly in Brazil. Developers and government officials maintain that the clearing must continue. They say that it is the only way to provide farmland to meet the needs of Brazil's rapidly expanding population. They know that cleared rain forest land can sustain agriculture for only four or five years, but they insist that this short-term solution is the only way to feed the people and help their nation escape from the poverty of the Third World. On the other hand, many environmentalists oppose further clearing. They note that the rainforest is home to a greater variety of species than any other ecosystem on earth. The environmentalists emphasize that most of these species face extinction as their rain forest habitat is destroyed. In addition, many scientists maintain that the vast plant growth in the rain forest plays a major role in cooling the planet — trees take up carbon dioxide and give off oxygen. They worry that cutting down our rain forests will speed up the trend toward global warming—sometimes called the "greenhouse effect."

As part of this symposium, we at the United Nations have asked for statements from representatives of each of the world's major religions. We have gathered you together—informed members of these religious communities—to discuss how your religious tradition would respond to the issue of rain forest depletion. We at the U.N. recognize that our position on this issue involves important religious questions about the relationship between God, humanity and the natural world. You are here because you are Jews from all over the world with an expertise or interest in the question of South American deforestation. We are looking to you to prepare the official Jewish statement for this symposium. We want to know what your tradition says about this important global question. You are a diverse group with differing opinions, interests and backgrounds regarding this issue. But we are asking you to do the difficult work of producing a unified statement about Judaism's response to this problem. Each of you will have a chance to present your own views and ideas. However, at the end of this session, your group as a whole will be asked how we should respond to this situation based on the Jewish traditions. We wish you the best of luck. The nations of the world, in fact, the planet itself, will benefit from your efforts. Thank you.

A Rainforest Roleplay

Role 1

Your Role: You are the only Jewish member of the Brazilian legislature. You believe that nothing is more important than the nation's immediate need for farmland to feed Brazil's people. You therefore support full-scale clearing of the rain forest.

Texts: You may use any texts from the quotes sheet. Be sure you can defend your choices. Some suggestions:

(1) In this quote, what do the words "master it" or "rule" imply about our rights regarding the rainforest?

(2) Given your character's position on the rain forest, how would you interpret the human responsibility to "keep it [the garden] and watch over it"?

(3) If the purpose of creation is to bring pleasure to the "guests" (human beings), how does that support your position about the rainforest?

(5) In this quote, the words "for your sake" seem to support your position about the rainforest. But will cutting down the rainforest "corrupt" the world beyond repair? Why would your character answer "no"?

Note: Be sure to look at the other quotations, since those who disagree with you will be using them to argue against you.

Role 2

Your Role: You are a wealthy American Jew who sits on the board of trustees of a major mining and development corporation. You feel that when the rain forest is cleared, it will open the way to lucrative (financially rewarding) mining contracts. This would, of course, be personally beneficial for you. But you also think that the money generated by this work would be highly beneficial to the Brazilian economy. You therefore support continued clearing.

Texts: You may use any texts from the quotes sheet. Be sure you can defend your choices. Some suggestions:

(1) In this quote, what do the words "master it" or "rule" imply about our rights regarding the rainforest?

(2) Given your character's position on the rain forest, how would you interpret the human responsibility to "keep it [the garden] and watch over it"?

(3) If the purpose of the creation is to bring pleasure to the "guests" (human beings), how does that support your position about the rainforest?

(5) In this quote, the words "for your sake" seem to support your position about the rainforest. But will cutting down the rainforest "corrupt" the world beyond repair? Why would your character answer "no"?

Note: Be sure to look at the other quotations, since those who disagree with you will be using them to argue against you.

Role 3

Your Role: You are a Jew from Rio who works for the Brazilian National Park Service. You share the view of many of your fellow citizens that Brazil's immediate economic need mandates development in most of the Amazon basin. However, you favor setting aside a fairly large portion of the rain forest as a national park and wildlife refuge. This would not save every endangered species in the rainforest from extinction, but it might preserve some species for a few decades.

Texts: You may use any texts from the quotes sheet. Be sure you can defend your choices. Some suggestions:

(2) Given your character's position on the rain forest, how would you interpret the human responsibility to "keep it [the garden] and watch over it?"

(4) How does this quote support your view that we have to attend to both the needs of human beings and the needs of other living things—that neither is more important that the other?

(12) Does your character embrace the philosophy of *bal tashchit*, the prohibition against needless destruction?

Note: Be sure to look at the other quotations, since those who disagree with you will be using them to argue against you.

Role 4

Your Role: You are an American Jew with a Ph.D. in agronomy (farm and crop management). You are currently employed by a multi-national corporation that provides equipment and advice to farmers and governments in the Third World. You are torn on this issue. On the one hand, you are concerned about the need for land and food to support the expanding Brazilian population. On the other hand, you know that any land created by clearing the rainforest will only sustain crops for four or five years before it erodes or turns into a "dust bowl." You are unsure whether to take a long-term or short-term approach.

Texts: You may use any texts from the quotes sheet. Be sure you can defend your choices. Some suggestions:

(5) This quote suggests that everything on earth is created for humanity's sake but that we must be careful not to abuse or corrupt this gift. How does this quote support your character's position?

(6) This quote makes our rights to the earth dependent on our merit—we have to be worthy of those rights. How might this quote affect your character's position?

(9) In this story, we learn of our responsibility to provide for future generations. How would your character weigh that long-term responsibility against our short-term responsibility to the present generation?

(12) You have learned about *bal tashchit*, the prohibition against needless destruction. You know that fruit trees should not be destroyed in war time. Now you must weigh how this law applies to rainforest trees in a time of peace.

Note: Be sure to look at the other quotations, since those who disagree with you will be using them to argue against you.

A Rainforest Roleplay

Role 5

Your Role: You are an Israeli *kibbutznik* with experience and expertise in the area of soil conservation. You are undecided on this matter. Because you have spent most of your life farming on your kibbutz, you are generally sympathetic to those who want to create more farmland. Yet you are aware of the limitations of the soil in the Amazon basin, which cannot sustain agriculture for even as long as a decade. You think it might be worth compromising and clearing part of the rainforest, since new technology may be developed which would allow farmers to sustain agriculture there for longer time periods. But you also suspect that it would be foolish to deforest most of the area on the basis of this hunch, when many nations currently produce more food than they consume and would be willing to ship food to meet the needs of the Brazilian people.

Texts: You may use any texts from the quotes sheet. Be sure you can defend your choices. Some suggestions:

(2) Given your character's position on the rainforest, how would you interpret the human responsibility "keep it [the garden] and watch over it?" How does your position enable humans to do both of these things at the same time?

(4) How does this quote support your view that we have to attend to both the needs of human beings and the needs of other living things—that neither is more important that the other?

(5) This quote suggests that everything on earth is created for humanity's sake but that we must be careful not to abuse or corrupt this gift. How does this quote support your character's position?

Note: Be sure to look at the other quotations, since those who disagree with you will be using them to argue against you.

Role 6

Your Role: You are a French Jewish chemist with a high-ranking job in a Paris-based pharmaceutical company. You are currently researching drugs that either cure or control certain kinds of cancer. Over the past twenty years, you have helped to develop many important drugs that represented major breakthroughs in health care. Over half of these drugs are derived from plants, herbs and insects found only in the Brazilian rain forest, where you do most of your field work. Therefore, you maintain that while the Brazilians may need to clear some of the forest, major deforestation could very likely wipe out species which might in the future have provided humanity with vital health benefits—perhaps even a cure for cancer.

Texts: You may use any texts from the quotes sheet. Be sure you can defend your choices. Some suggestions:

(5) This quote suggests that everything on earth is created for humanity's sake but that we must be careful not to abuse or corrupt this gift. How does this quote support your character's position?

(7) How does this quote reinforce your concern over losing the natural resources for medicines in the rainforest? How does this quote help us look differently at the value of the life forms that depend upon the rain forest?

(11) As with #7, how does this quote suggest we view the natural resources and life forms that depend upon the rain forest habitat to survive?

Note: Be sure to look at the other quotations, since those who disagree with you will be using them to argue against you.

Role 7

Your Role: You are a Jewish botanist at Oxford University in England. Every summer, you spend time in the Amazon Basin conducting scientific studies of plant pathology. You oppose any further deforestation of the area, since this activity would undoubtedly wipe out several rare species of plants that neither you nor any of your colleagues have had the chance to study.

Texts: You may use any texts from the quotes sheet. Be sure you can defend your choices. Some suggestions:

(5) This quote suggests that we should be careful about how we treat the earth because if we make a mess of it, there will be no one to correct our mistakes. How does the warning not to do irreversible damage support your character's viewpoint?

(7) This quote suggests that every species is here for a purpose, even if we're not clear on what that purpose is. How might your character use this quote to support the idea that future research of endangered species could be beneficial to human beings in ways we cannot see now?

Note: Be sure to look at the other quotations, since those who disagree with you will be using them to argue against you.

Role 8

Your Role: You are a Syrian Jewish nature writer and ecologist. You oppose any further deforestation, not because it would wipe out species with potential value for humanity, but rather because you believe that each species, from single-celled plants to beetles, to monkeys, has a right to exist for its own sake. You think the earth itself is a living thing, and you claim that people are just one very small part of the whole world, no more worthy or important than any other part.

Texts: You may use any texts from the quotes sheet. Be sure you can defend your choices. Some suggestions:

(4) Does Maimonides agree with you? What benefit does he see in taking this perspective?

(7) This quote suggests that every species is here for a purpose, even if we're not always clear on what that purpose is. Also according to this quote, God gave each species a purpose, and not every purpose serves human beings' needs. How does this view support your position?

(10) How does the idea that human beings belong to the land (and not vice-versa) reinforce your character's position that we do not have the right to do whatever we want with the land? What do you think the story means when it says that human beings "belong" to the land?

(12) How would you apply *bal tashchit*, the prohibition against needless destruction, to the rainforests?

Note: Be sure to look at the other quotations, since those who disagree with you will be using them to argue against you.

Jewish Sources

1) And God created humanity in the Divine Image...they were created male and female. God blessed them, saying: "Be fertile and multiply, fill the earth and master it; rule over the fish of the ocean and the birds of the sky and all the wild things that creep on the land."
—Genesis 1:27-28

2) God placed the human in the garden of Eden to serve and keep it.
—Genesis 2:15

3) God said [to the angels]: "Why was everything, sheep and oxen, the birds of the sky, and the fish of the ocean....created? The owner of a tall building filled with good things and no guest [to enjoy them] would feel little pleasure in the bounty of it. [Humanity is the guest for whom the bounty is there to be enjoyed.]"
—Genesis Rabbah 8:6

4) Do not believe that all things exist for the sake of humanity. On the contrary, one must believe that...everything exists for its own sake and not for anything or anyone else. When one knows one's own soul without erring, one can understand all beings as they are and [so] achieve calm and serene thoughts.
—Maimonides, Guide of the Perplexed III:14

5) Upon creating the first human beings, God guided them around the Garden of Eden, saying: "Look at my creations! See how beautiful and perfect they are! I created everything for you. Make sure you don't ruin or devastate My world. If you do, there will be no one after you to fix it."
—Ecclesiastes Rabbah 7:13

6) "And have dominion over the fish of the ocean, the birds of the sky, and all the living things that creep on the earth." (Genesis 1:28). Rabbi Hanina said: "Humanity will rule over them if they deserve to; if they do not deserve to, then they will go under [and be ruled by the evil they have created]."
—Genesis Rabbah 8:12

7) "The Rabbis said: Even though you may think them superfluous in this world, creatures such as flies, bugs and gnats, have their allotted task in the scheme of creation, as it says "And God saw everything that God had made, and behold, it was very good," (Genesis1:31)."
—Genesis Rabbah 10:7

8) It is forbidden to live in a city that does not have greenery.
—Jerusalem *Talmud, Kiddushin* 12:12

9) While the sage, Choni, was walking along a road, he saw a man planting a carob tree. Choni asked him: "How long will it take for this tree to bear fruit?"

"Seventy years," replied the man.

Choni then asked: "Are you so healthy a man that you expect to live that length of time and eat its fruit?"

The man answered: "I found a fruitful world because my ancestors planted it for me. Likewise I am planting for my children."
—Babylonian *Talmud, Taanit* 23a

10) Two men were fighting over a piece of land. Each claimed ownership. To resolve their differences, they agreed to put the case before the rabbi. The rabbi listened but could not come to a decision. Finally, he said, "Since I cannot decide to whom this land belongs, let us ask the land." He put his ear to the ground, then straightened up. "Gentlemen, the land says that it belongs to neither of you — but that you belong to it."
—Jewish folk tale

11) Rabbi Huna taught: Everything within sight is part of the Holy Blessed God's pathways.
—Genesis Rabbah 12:1

12) Whoever breaks vessels or rips up garments, destroys a building, stops up a fountain, or ruin food is guilty of violating the prohibition of *bal tashchit*.
—Babylonian *Talmud, Kiddushin* 32a

A Rainforest Roleplay

Character Development Worksheet

Instructions: Read your character description, including the Jewish texts that support your character's position. Make sure you understand how and why those particular quotes support your character's viewpoint. Use the following questions to organize your opening statement. You will read your statement to the other members of your group.

1. Who are you (your character) and why are you interested in the fate of the rainforests?

My name is _____ and I am at this conference because

2. What is your character's position regarding the rainforest?

I believe that

3. What reasons can you give for your position?

I suggest we take this approach to the rainforests because

4. What Jewish teachings support your position?

My position on the rainforest issue is supported by Jewish teachings. Let me refer to some specific Jewish texts that demonstrate why I think this is the right "Jewish" answer. (Read some of the selected quotes and explain how they support your character's view.)

A Rainforest Roleplay

A Rainforest Roleplay

United Nations Rainforest Symposium: Report of the Jewish Delegation

Sub-Committee Letter

1. Our Recommendation:

2. Our Reasons:

3. Jewish quotes that led us this conclusion and how they support our position (you may use the numbers to refer to quotations rather than writing them out):

SUPPLEMENTARY ACTIVITY

Tu B'Shvat, the Jewish New Year of the Trees

Tu B'Shvat is a wonderful holiday that celebrates the trees and all of nature. What follows is background information about the holiday and a framework for a *Tu B'Shvat seder* (a ritual meal). The *Kabbalists* (certain Jewish mystics) believed that one way we can fix the world is through our prayers and celebrations. *Be sure to honor this in some way!* Allow yourself plenty of time to prepare for the seder. *Tu B'Shvat* is definitely a holiday whose time has come!

History of *Tu B'Shvat*

The Jewish calendar is a lunar one; the holidays mark the phases of the moon. *Tu B' Shvat*, the Jewish New Year of the Trees, falls on the full moon of *Shvat,* which is the fifteenth (in Hebrew *"tu"*) of that month. Legend has it that the trees requested this mid-winter date from the Creator for their New Year because they realized that only after the winter rains had fallen could they flower and sprout new growth. *Tu B'Shvat*, then, is the time to honor the trees, the waters that nourish the trees, as well as the essence of all creation: the Tree of Life.

Tu B' Shvat was originally a tithing day, a day to pay taxes on the fruit trees. This date was established as a way of marking the age of trees because in order to fulfill the obligations of Jewish agricultural law, it was important to know to which year the fruits belonged.

In the tenth century, Rabbenu Gershom, the leading rabbinic authority of the time, prohibited public fasts on *Tu B'Shvat*. In the eleventh century, a set of psalms were composed for the *Shmoneh Esreh* prayers (the 18 Benedictions) on *Tu B'Shvat*. By the sixteenth century, Rabbi Issachar Sussman had noted that it was common practice among central European Jews to eat fifteen types of fruit in honor of the name *"Tu"* (15).

Tu B'Shvat was a relatively minor holiday until the 1600s, when it sparked the interest of the *Kabbalists,* a group of Jewish mystics. In their love for God and God's presence in nature, they created a *tikkun*, a repairing of the world, to honor this day. Their celebration took the form of a *seder,* an ordered ritual. They recited blessings and feasted on fruit and wine. They drank four cups of wine to symbolize the seasons: white wine for winter, white with a drop of red for spring, red with a drop of white for summer, and full red for autumn. Their fruit feast celebrated the vast variety of species. The variety and abundance of fruit were a reminder of God's creativity. In addition to feasting, they studied passages from Jewish texts that illuminated God's presence in nature.

156

Each fruit in the feast required the recitation of a blessing, so eating many kinds of fruit provided an opportunity to recite a multitude of blessings. This was important, because blessings carried great weight for the *Kabbalists*. They believed blessings were a direct link between people's positive intentions and the healing of the earth. The more blessings they recited, the greater repair would take place in the world. They believed that blessings insured the continuity of the divine flow in the world, and thereby sustenance for future generations.

The *Kabbalists* assembled readings from Jewish texts that expressed divinity in nature. These texts, along with the instructions for selecting the representative fruits and wines and their blessings, make up the *Pri Etz Hadar* (*The Fruit of the Goodly Tree*), the *Kabbalistic* guide to the celebration of *Tu B'Shvat*.

As the *Pri Etz Hadar* was widely distributed, communities around the world began to develop their own customs for celebrating the New Year of the Trees. In Bucharia and Kurdistan, the holiday was known as "The Day of Eating the Seven Species" (see Deuteronomy 8:8), and a feast of thirty kinds of fruit was prepared. In India, the use of fifty varieties of fruits makes for an abundant feast! In rural Morocco, the richer Jews would invite the whole town to their homes and fill the guests' hats with fruit. In Persia, it was customary to climb onto neighbors' roofs and lower an empty basket through the chimney. The basket would be returned laden with fruit. In Persia and Afghanistan, Jews purchased new fabrics on *Tu B'Shvat* from which clothing for *Pesach* was sewn.

There was a wide-spread custom of eating jelly made from the *etrog* (ritual citrus fruit) of the previous *Sukkot* and praying for fine quality *etrogim* for the coming *Sukkot*.

In Salonica, Greece, legend had it that on *Tu B'Shvat* an angel tapped the head of every plant, commanding, "Grow!" Another Greek legend related that on this day, the trees embrace. All those who witnessed this miraculous event would have a wish fulfilled.

Some barren Jewish women, believing in the power of sympathetic magic, would plant raisins and candy near trees on *Tu B'Shvat* night, praying for fertility. Young girls eligible for marriage were brought to trees where an imitation marriage was enacted. If shortly afterward, buds were found on the trees where they were "married," they knew their turn would soon come.

In some areas, *Tu B'Shvat* celebrations were held in the homes of families who had lost a loved one during the past year to remind them of the prohibition of mourning on that day. The renewal of a tree's life was considered parallel to the resurrection.

Today, in modern Israel, tree-planting ceremonies take place throughout the land on Tu B'Shvat. Jews from around the world participate in this effort by contributing money for the purchase of trees. During the past two decades many North American Jews, in their commitment to enrich their Jewish practice, celebrate *Tu B'Shvat* with their own versions of the *Kabbalistic seder*.

Because there is no set liturgy for the holiday, *Tu B' Shvat* readily lends itself to creative interpretation. People of all ages can participate in making a *Tu B'Shvat* seder using the readings listed below from the original *Pri Etz Hadar* and adding their own. The critical elements of the *seder* are blessing and tasting fruits and wines and reciting prayers that encourage our remembrance of God's presence in the natural world.

Symbolism of the *Tu B'Shvat* Seder

Four worlds

The *Kabbalists'* perspective on life grew out of a four-fold understanding; they saw four layers of reality. These layers are referred to as "worlds".

Assiyah: World of Action. This is the outer shell of reality. It is the physical world: the soil beneath our feet, the **earth** on which we live.

Yetzirah: World of Emotion or Formation. This is the world of our feelings. It is the fountain or **well** from which our creativity flows.

Briyah: World of Thought and Creation. This is the power of intention. Our thoughts are like the **air**; we can not see them, yet they have real life and substance. God created the whole world by "speaking" thoughts.

Atzilut: World of Spirit. This is the world of the mystery, the divine energy in all things, the eternal cycle of life, the **fire** of transformation.

Four cups of wine

The four different cups of wine represent the four seasons: white for winter, pale pink (white with a bit of red mixed in) for spring, light red (red with a bit of white mixed in) for summer, and dark, full red for autumn. The four cups may also be said to signify the four elements of the *Kabbalists'* world view.

Three types of fruit

There are three types of fruits, symbolizing three of the four *Kabbalistic* worlds. Fruits symbolic of *Assiyah* have a hard, inedible skin or shell covering the edible section: oranges, grapefruits, melons, pomegranates, almonds, bananas, etc. Fruits symbolic of *Yetzirah* have inedible pits or seeds inside: dates, olives, plums, apples, pears, etc. Fruits symbolic of *Briyah* are entirely edible: figs, raisins, blueberries, grapes, strawberries, etc. *Atzilut,* the world of the spirit, is not symbolized by any fruit.

There are several explanations for the three groupings of these fruits. Some propose that the first group suggests the protective coverings we need in winter, the second

158

reminds us of the miracle of rebirth—through its seeds—which occurs each spring, and the third resembles the soft dream-like state of summer.

Others maintain that the hard-shelled fruits represent the child in the mother's womb, the fruits with pits are like young people who are as hard as the seed but still need outside protection, and the entirely edible fruits represent adults who can care for themselves inside and out. Feel free to add your own interpretations.

Fifteen varieties of fruit

Most *Tu B'Shvat* seders also include the eating of fifteen varieties of fruits and vegetables, among them the seven species that are grown in Israel. Fifteen corresponds to the date *"Tu"*, the fifteenth (of the Hebrew month of *Shvat*).

A *Tu B'Shvat Seder*

This is one possible version of the *seder*. It is designed to be an elegant four-course dinner of fruits and wines, with readings, songs, and discussion accompanying each course. The first course will be the *Assiyah*, next the *Yetzirah*, then the *Briyah*, and last, the *Atzilut* (though no fruit is eaten for this course, as this is the world of pure spirit).

Preparations

Fruits: Select five fruits from each of the categories. Have enough so that everyone can have a taste of each. And try and have at least one kind of fruit that no one has eaten in at least thirty days so that they may recite the *She'hechiyanu* (renewal) blessing. Cut the fruits up into bitesize pieces, leaving the core or shell intact, so that participants will be able to experience the symbolism of the food.

Place the fruits from the same categories together on a platter or in a bowl. Arrange the fruits in a way that is aesthetically pleasing to you. You can think of each category of fruits as one course in a four-course dinner.

Wine: Provide both red and white wine or grape juice.

Utensils: Use non-disposable plates and clean them up when you finish. It would be inappropriate to use disposables at a festival honoring trees and our environment. Decorate the room for the occasion. Set tables with tablecloths, candles and flowers.

Readings and music: Select in advance about ten different readings for each world. Have a variety of contemporary texts as well as traditional Jewish sources. Use appropriate texts from this book, as well as others you have chosen. Also select a song or dance for each world. Assign a volunteer to each reading or activity, or have members of the group select their own readings. Make sure each world is represented.

Blessings: You will need to recite a blessing for the fruits and wine of each world

The blessing that is recited before consuming fruit grown on trees is:

ברוך אתה ד׳ אלקינו מלך העולם בורא פרי האץ.

Baruch Atah Adonai Eloheynu Melech Ha-olam Boray pree ha-etz.

Praise to You *Adonai*, our God and Universal Ruler Who creates the fruit of the tree.

The blessing that is recited before consuming fruit that grows close to the ground (i.e.: strawberries and bananas) is:

ברוך אתה ד׳ אלקינו מלך העולם בורא פרי האדמה.

Baruch Atah Adonai Eloheynu Melech Ha-olam Boray pree ha-adamah.

Praise to You *Adonai*, our God and Universal Ruler Who creates the fruit of the ground.

If the fruit is "new" (ie: if you have not tasted this fruit yet this season) you may recite this blessing over it as well (in addition to one of the blessings above):

ברוך אתה ד׳ אלקינו מלך העולם שהחיינו, וקימנו, והגיענו לזמן הזה.

Baruch Atah Adonai Eloheynu Melech Ha-olam she'hechiyanu v'kiyimanu v'higiyanu lazman ha-zeh.

Praise to You *Adonai*, our God and Universal Ruler Who has kept us alive, sustained us and brought us to this season.

The blessing to be recited over wine or grape juice is:

ברוך אתה ד׳ אלקינו מלך העולם בורא פרי הגפן.

Baruch Atah Adonai Eloheynu Melech Ha-olam Boray pree ha-gafen.

Praise to You *Adonai*, our God and Universal Ruler Who creates the fruit of the vine.

When you have finished your *seder,* recite the blessings after eating. They can be found in any standard prayerbook.

And God said: Let the waters under the heavens be gathered together, and let the dry land appear, and it was so. And God called the dry land Earth, and the gathering together of the waters God called Seas. And God saw that it was good. And God said: Let the earth bring forth grass, herb yielding seed, and fruit tree yielding fruit after its kind, whose seed is in itself, upon the earth. And it was so. . . And God saw that it was good. And there was evening and there was morning, a third day.
—Genesis 1:9-13

All the commandments which I command you this day shall you observe, that you may live, and multiply, and go in and possess the land which *Adonai* swore to your ancestors. And you shall remember all the way which *Adonai* your God led you these forty years in the wilderness, to humble you, and to prove you, to know what was in your heart, whether you would keep God's commandments, or not. . . . Therefore you shall keep the commandments of *Adonai* your God, to walk in God's ways, and to look in awe on God. For *Adonai* your God brings you into a good land, a land of water courses, of fountains and depths that spring out of valleys and hills; a land of wheat, and barley, and vines, and fig trees, and pomegranates; a land of olive oil, and honey; a land in which you shall eat bread without scarceness, you shall not lack any thing; a land in which the stones are iron, and out of whose hills you may dig brass. When you have eaten and are satisfied, then you shall bless *Adonai* your God for the good land which God has given you.
—Deuteronomy 8:1-10

If you walk in my statutes, and keep my commandments, and do them; then I will give you rain in its season, and the land will give its produce, and the trees of the field will give their fruit. And your threshing will reach to the vintage, and the vintage shall reach to the sowing time: and you will eat your bread to the full, and dwell in your land safely. And I will give peace in the land, and you will lie down, and none will make you afraid.... For I will turn myself to you, and make you fruitful and establish a covenant with you. And you will eat old store, and remove the old because of the new. And I will set my tabernacle among you: and my soul will not abhor you. And I will walk among you, and will be your God, and you will be my people. I am *Adonai* your God, who brought you out of the land of Egypt, that you should not be their bondsmen; and I have broken the bonds of your yoke, and made you walk upright.
—Leviticus 26:3-13

MATERIALS & PREPARATIONS
•Plant containers, soil, and small rocks; or, a garden area
•Hand tools such as trowels, shovels, spades, or spading forks if you have actual garden areas; watering cans or hoses
•Seeds

A Garden Project

Wherever we live, even in the cities, we can be in touch with nature and the seasons. This project will enable participants to experience nature by being directly involved in the process of growing things. Jewish tradition tells us when to plant certain crops, when to harvest them, and what their significance is (for the land of Israel). We also learn to refrain from harvesting all our crops; we leave the produce in the corners of our fields for those who have none.

You will need a place to garden: a sunny windowsill, small planting beds along a sidewalk or building, a garden plot, or containers on a patio or roof. Alternatively, you may decide to get involved in a garden project that is already established, such as a community garden or an interfaith group that raises food for the local soup kitchen. Participants can also take these ideas home and begin their own gardens.

If you are container-gardening, you will need potting soil, and some gravel to put in the bottom of containers to help drain water. Containers for gardening can be found in many unexpected places. Check with a community garden or a landscaping business to see if they will donate some used containers instead of throwing them away. Old buckets and coffee cans work well if you punch some holes near the bottom for drainage. Some hand tools will be useful, although large spoons are sufficient. You will need a watering can that will be gentle on seedlings. And of course, you will need seeds.

Garden supply businesses, botanical gardens and arboreta, and other gardening organizations can offer helpful suggestions.

You may want to share some of your harvest with soup kitchens, senior centers, food banks, or other similar services and organizations. You will want to use your harvest to expand your celebration of several holidays, such as Passover and *Sukkot*.

Sukkot, September/October

Sukkot is the autumn harvest festival. *Sukkah* refers to the little open air hut our ancestors built for protecting their crops after they harvested them from the field; it is also a reminder of the temporary huts our ancestors built in their wanderings in the desert.

Sukkot is the holiday of joy. If you grow vegetables for your autumn harvest and for decorating your *sukkah*, you will see why! *Sukkot* will soon become your favorite holiday.

Sukkot is the time to harvest all the vegetables that you planted in the spring and summer. You can grow corn for the corn stalks to make the *s'chach* for the *sukkah*'s roof. You can grow squash, gourds and pumpkins to decorate your *sukkah*. Corn, gourds, squash, and pumpkins are truly **simple** to grow. Make sure you prepare your soil and get your seeds in before July 1 for an October harvest. Try planting a variety of gourds for different colors and shapes. Gourds and pumpkins make great candle holders. Rabbi Everett Gendler, who has perfected the art of farming with the holidays, suggests "*Ya'akov* O'Lanterns". Try out your artistic talent and create your own. Bring a special light to your *sukkah*.

S'chach, the thatch that makes the *sukkah*'s roof, must be green. Spread out your corn stalks over top of your *sukkah* so you can see the stars at night from inside—this is the law! If you do not harvest your corn for eating, you can use it for decorations. It will be part of the decor—just peel back the husks. Indian corn makes beautiful decorations. Let some of your corn dry out and then try popping it. You can string the popped corn and hang it in your *sukkah* for more festive decorations.

Sukkot is also the time to plant a winter grain crop for harvesting at Passover. Try planting a planter box of wheat on a windowsill if you live in a cold climate.

Channukah, December

It is traditional to eat latkes, potato pancakes, on this holiday. Try growing potatoes in containers—big pots grow big potatoes, little pots grow tiny potatoes. Potatoes will need to be planted in late September to be ripe for *Channukah*.

Tu B'Shvat, January/February

At *Tu B'Shvat* it is customary to plant parsley to harvest for the Passover *seder* plate. Parsley can be easily grown on a windowsill.

Some people enjoy planting their own horseradish for the *seder* plate as well. Check with a garden supply store to find out how long it takes to grow in your area, and whether you can plant it outside. Horseradish will grow in indoor containers, too.

Tu B'Shvat is also an ideal time to start seeds in your house for spring vegetables and flowers.

Passover, *March/April*

If you grew parsley or horseradish at *Tu B'Sh'vat*, it should be ready now for your Passover *seder* plate. Passover is also the time to harvest your winter wheat. At *Pesach*, during the time of the Temple, our ancestors made an offering of their winter grain.

Pesach marks the beginning of spring. From *Pesach* to *Shavuot*, it's time to plant a variety of vegetables and flowers. Passover is also the time to plant your spring wheat for harvest at *Shavuot.*

Shavuot, *May/June*

Shavuot is a holiday in which we traditionally decorate our synagogues and homes with cut flowers and plants in bloom. Gather flowers and branches and greenery from your garden.

By now, your spring crop of wheat should be ready to harvest. Our ancestors used to bake two loaves of bread from the first crop of spring wheat. They made an offering of the loaves at the Temple. This offering of bread symbolized the gift of God's wheat and the work of human hands.

MATERIALS & PREPARATION
- Copy of texts for each particpant.
- Before beginning, you will need to make animal picture cards. Simply take old copies of nature magazines , cut out pictures of birds, insects, fish and animals, and tape them to index cards.

Compassion for Animals

Walk like an Animal ▲▲

It is preferable to do this activity outdoors, but it can be done indoors as well. Divide the group into subgroups (of 8-10) people and give each person an animal picture card. As you pass out the cards, explain that the players should keep the identity of their animal secret.

When the game starts, each person in each group takes a turn portraying their animal. The "actor" should begin by capturing the animal's character in a still pose and holding the pose for eight seconds. Then she should move like the animal. To end the performance she can make the animal's sound. When the actor has finished, everyone else in the group tries to guess their animal. Keep playing until everyone has had a turn to act. It would be a good idea for the leader to participate in this activity. Older teens and adults can have a good time with this activity and still learn by allowing them to really "ham it up".

Text Study: *Tzaar Baalei Chayyim* ▲▲▲

The Jewish sages spoke at length about the human obligation toward the members of the animal kingdom. At a time when many treated animals ruthlessly, they established the *mitzvah* of *tzaar baalei chayyim*—compassion for the pain of all living creatures.

Pass out copies of Jewish texts on *tzaar baalei chayyim* to all participants (see Readings & Worksheets). Have the group sit in a circle as volunteers read the texts out loud. Alternatively, you may choose to divide the class up into small groups; if so, assign each group a few texts and have them answer the questions on their worksheet. After ten minutes, have the group reconvene and ask individuals to share their texts and discussions with the other participants. Use the Leader's Worksheet sheet as a guide for the discussion.

Bringing It Home ▲

In Judaism, there is a sense of obligation and compassion toward animals. Judaism has traditionally mandated compassion to animals as the *mitzvah* of *tzaar baalei chayyim*. Generally, this *mitzvah* tries to balance legitimate human use of animals and animal products with the serious demand that we avoid causing "needless" pain and suffering.

Compassion for Animals

Text Study: *Tzaar Baalei Chayyim*

Reading

When you see the donkey of your enemy couching under its burden and you would rather not help him raise it, you must nevertheless raise it with him.
—Exodus 23:5

The seventh day is a Sabbath of the Eternal your God: you shall not do any work — you, your son or your daughter, your male or female servant, your ox or your donkey or any of your cattle. . .
—Deuteronomy 5:14

Do not boil a [goat] kid in its mother's milk.
—Deuteronomy 14:21

If, on your way you happen upon a bird's nest in a tree or on the ground, with the baby birds or eggs in it , and the mother is sitting over the fledglings or on the eggs, do not take the mother with her young. Let the mother go and take only the young. This way you will fare well and have a long life.
—Deuteronomy 22:6-7

Do not plow with an ox and a donkey together.
—Deuteronomy 22:10

If an animal falls into a ditch [on the Sabbath], bring pillows and bedding and place them under it [for it cannot be removed until after the Sabbath ends].
—Babylonian *Talmud, Shabbat* 128b

Rabbi Judah HaNasi watched a calf being led to slaughter. The animal broke from the herd and hid itself under the rabbi's clothing, crying for mercy. But he pushed it away saying, "Go! For you were destined for this!" They said in heaven, "Since he showed no compassion, let us bring suffering upon him." For years afterwards, the rabbi suffered from a series of painful illnesses. One day his servant was sweeping the house. She was about to sweep away some young weasels she found lying on the floor. "Leave them alone!" he said to her. Then they said of him in heaven, "Since he has shown compassion, let us be compassionate with him," and he was cured.
—Babylonian *Talmud, Baba Metzia* 85a

. . . When animals lose their young, their pain is very great. There is no difference between the pain of humans and the pain of other living beings. The love and tenderness of the mother comes from the heart, not the intellect, and this capacity exists not only in humans but in most living beings. . .
—Maimonides, *Guide of the Perplexed*, III:48

The dietary laws, whose purposes and meanings, unexplained in the Bible, have been disputed for generations, have one core idea throughout. In their prohibitions against eating blood, or the flesh of living animals, in their restrictions on the kinds and parts of animals that may be consumed, they set limits on human dominance over the animal world.
—Klagsbrun, F. *Voices of Wisdom* , p.450

166

Compassion for Animals

Text Study: *Tzaar Baalei Chayyim*

Participant Worksheet

1. Do you think most people are inclined to offer help to their enemy's animals? Why is this commanded?

2. Should the mandate that one's ox, donkey, and cattle be free from work on *Shabbat* be extended to other animals (such as horses, dogs, etc.)? What do you think constitutes "work" for an animal?

3. Francine Klagsbrun speaks about the dietary laws (including not boiling a calf in its mother's milk) as setting limits on human dominance over animals. In fact, according to the Torah, before Noah every human being was a vegetarian. Some Jews believe that it was only as a concession to human frailty and moral weakness that God let us eat meat at all. Speak about the importance of diet. Do you believe it is more moral to be a vegetarian? To at least observe some of the kosher laws if you do choose to eat meat?

Also note the link to ecology: meat-eating consumes vast amounts of natural resources. Growing grains, fruits, and vegetables uses less than 5 percent as much of the raw materials as does meat production. By eating less meat, one actually puts less strain on the environment, helps feed the world—and saves a cow or two as well!

4. Do you agree with Maimonides' claim that animals are capable of feeling great emotional pain and distress? What evidence do you have to support your position?

5. What led Rabbi Judah HaNasi to become more compassionate and why?

6. Based on these texts, what do you think Judaism would say about the question of using animals for research?

Compassion for Animals

Text Study: *Tzaar Baalei Chayyim*

Leader Worksheet

1. Do you think most people are inclined to offer help to their enemy's animals? Why is this commanded?
Most people would probably take joy in anything which troubles their enemies. This commandment reminds us that although this may be natural, we must not let the enmity between humans blot out our compassion for the innocent, suffering animal.

2. Should the mandate that one's ox, donkey, and cattle be free from work on *Shabbat* be extended to other animals (such as horses, dogs, etc.)? What do you think constitutes "work" for an animal?
The mandate not to work on Shabbat *does extend to all animals. In the case of animals, work really consists of putting them to labor for human purposes (plowing , etc). Such work must always be done humanely; hence, plowing with an ox and a donkey together is prohibited. But on* Shabbat, *the animals, too, get a total rest.*

3. Francine Klagsbrun speaks about the dietary laws (including not boiling a calf in its mother's milk) as setting limits on human dominance over animals. In fact, according to the Torah, before Noah every human being was a vegetarian. Some Jews believe that it was only as a concession to human frailty and moral weakness that God let us eat meat at all. Speak about the importance of diet. Do participants believe it is more moral to be a vegetarian? To at least observe some of the kosher laws if they do choose to eat meat?

Also note the link to ecology: meat-eating consumes vast amounts of natural resources. Growing grains, fruits, and vegetables uses less than 5 percent as much of the raw materials as does meat production. By eating less meat, one demands less of the environment.

4. Do you agree with Maimonides' claim that animals are capable of feeling great emotional pain and distress? What evidence do you have to support your position?
Encourage those participants with pets to share stories which show that animals have definite "moods," feel emotional distress, etc.

5. What led Rabbi Judah HaNasi to become more compassionate and why?
His own series of illnesses seems to have made him aware of the power of suffering and its grip over all living things. As a young man, he was callous; his personal pain taught him to be kind.

6. Based on these texts, what do you think Judaism would say about the question of using animals for research?
This is a complex and important question. In general, Jewish tradition does allow us to use animals for the purpose of benefitting humankind. Hence we can wear leather, employ animals in farm labor and, as we have seen, eat some species (provided that the dietary rules are observed). On the other hand, we have also seen that the

tradition provides strict guidelines on how we use animals—humane treatment, allowing them to rest one day a week and above all, sensitivity to their pain. Ask participants how they would balance these two elements and what position they would take. Generally, most Jewish commentators would probably allow animal research that is medically necessary in order to save human lives, but would be wary of superfluous research that harms animals. They would also insist upon conditions which do all they can to minimize the animals' pain and suffering.

Glossary of Hebrew and Jewish Terms

adam	Earthling; person; as in Adam, the first man
adamah	Earth
Adonai	One of God's names
aggadah	From the Hebrew for "telling"; non-legal Rabbinic writings; Jewish folklore
bal tashchit	The injunction "do not destroy"
brachah	Blessing; *brachot* (pl.)
brit	Covenant; a binding contract with the Divine
Channukah	Jewish holiday marking the victory of the Hasmoneans (Maccabees) over Hellenism and the miracle of an oil lamp that lasted seven days longer than it should have
Haggadah	The basic text for the Pasover seder
hevrutah	Pair of students studying (Jewish texts) together; *hevrutot* (pl.)
Kabbalist	Type of Jewish mystic; from *Kabbalah*, literally "received"
kal v'homer	Literally, from easy to hard; a rabbinic interpretive tool
kavannah	From the Hebrew "to direct"; usually used to mean intentionality in performing a *mitzvah* or while praying
Midrash	From the Hebrew "to seek" or "to interpret" (see *aggadah*)
Mishnah	A terse compendium of mostly legal material from the earliest strata of Rabbinic Judaism, compiled around the year 200 C.E.
mitzvah	Commandment; obligation; *mitzvot* (pl.)
Pesach	Passover; Jewish holiday commemerating the exodus from Egypt and marking the beginning of spring
Rosh Hodesh	The new month, new moon
seder	Literally "order"; used to designate the (ordered) ritual meal of Passover and *Tu B'shvat*
Sh'ma	Shorthand for the "Hear O Israel" prayer, central prayer proclaiming a Jew's faith in God's Oneness
sh'virat ha-kaylim	Breaking of the vessels (*Kabbalistic*)
Shabbat	The sabbath
She'vee'it	Sabbatical year; every seventh year when Jews in the land of Israel are commanded to let their land lie fallow
shomer(et) adamah	Keeper of the earth (m./f.); *shomrei adamah* (pl.)
sukkah	Ritual open-air hut (booth) used during *Sukkot* (pl. *sukkah*)
Sukkot	Fall harvest holiday where Jews are commanded to sit in *sukkot*
Talmud	Compendium of material from the post-*Mishnaic* Rabbinic Jews, an elaboration on the material in the *Mishnah* and many pages of tangents; Palestinian (Jerusalem) version compiled around the year 400 CE. and the Babylonian version redacted around the year 500 C.E.
tikkun olam	A *kabbalistic* concept; literally "repairing the world"
tikkun	Repair; mend; fix
Torah	Literally "to teach" or "teacher"; the Bible, the act of studying
Tu B'Shvat	15th of the Hebrew month Shvat, celebrated as the New Year for the trees
Tza'ar Baalei Chayyim	Principle of showing compassion for the pain of all living creatures
tzedakah	Literally "righteousness"; the pursuit of a just society; charity
yovel	Jubilee; 50th year in the Jewish agricultural cycle

An Opinionated Guide to Environmental Resources

by Jonathan Schorsch

An opinionated guide to environmental groups and resources here, there and everywhere. Given that there are some 5,000 groups in the United States alone, we've chosen those that we feel are the most important, useful or unique. Readers should keep in mind that many of the larger national groups maintain offices in several cities. Some of the information here is extracted from material provided by the groups themselves.

THE "BIG TEN"

The "Big Ten" is an unofficial title for the largest U.S. environmental organizations. Because the grouping is informal, there is no agreement on who is included and who is not!

Environmental Defense Fund
257 Park Avenue S.
New York, NY 10010
(212) 505-2100

Established in 1967, EDF has grown to include some 150,000 members nationwide. With its staff of lawyers, scientists and economists EDF works to protect and improve environmental quality and public health. Considered slightly conservative for an activist group, EDF has nontheless proven very effective in bringing litigation to ensure strong environmental legislation, exchanging expertise with (former) Soviet environmental scientists, and offering workable solutions to problems of pollution, recycling, ozone depletion, the greenhouse effect, and other critical issues.

Greenpeace
1436 U Street, NW
Washington, DC 20009
(202) 462-1177

Begun in 1971 in British Columbia by a small group of people opposed to nuclear testing on Amchitka Island in Alaska, Greenpeace gained its reputation for dramatic, non-violent protest and action: dropping banners from smokestacks, interrupting naval maneuvers, and harassing nuclear testers. Today, Greenpeace International has offices in over 20 countries and claims some 2.3 million members, making it the world's largest environmental organization. Greenpeace's current campaigns and efforts are too numerous to mention, but include efforts to approach zero toxic emission, to help Native Americans protect their lands from industrial encroachment, to stop production of ozone-depleting chlorofluorocarbons (CFCs), to halt the killing of dolphins in tuna fishing, and of course, to stop nuclear production. Greenpeace information publications are relied upon by activists and others around the world.

National Audubon Society
950 Third Avenue
New York, NY 10022
(212) 832-3200

Founded in 1905 to oppose the killing of plumed birds for use of their feathers in women's hats, the organization has come a long way since then. Today this "voice of reason" focuses on a wide range of conservation issues: plants, animals and habitats, but also land and water use, energy policies, pollution and issues of global import. With over half a million members and local chapters throughout the states, it's probable that there's an Audubon reserve or bird sanctuary near you. The group is also known for its wide range of ecology travel tours, educational programs and activities, its lobbying and its research. Its television specials continue the marvelous aesthetic appreciation of nature begun by founder John James Audubon, whose romanticized bird paintings are world-renowned.

National Wildlife Federation
1400 Sixteenth St., NW
Washington, DC 20036-2266
(202) 797-6800

The largest environmental organization in the country, NWF claims some 5.6 members and 52 affiliates. Its main emphasis is the wise use of our natural resources, accomplished through a variety of means, including educational programs, publications, research and lobbying. Children are probably familiar with NWF's *Ranger Rick* and *Your Big Backyard* magazines, while adults may know one of their seven resource conservation centers. The Federation also helped establish the Atchafalaya National Wildlife Refuge in Louisiana. Newer developments include the creation of the National Biotechnology Policy Center, which focuses on the environmental implications of biotechnology. NWF offers "conservation summits" for educators and nature enthusiasts of all ages.

Natural Resources Defense Council
40 West 20th Street
New York, NY 10011
(212) 727-2700

Founded in 1970 by a bunch of Yale School alumni, NRDC is a major force in environmental litigation, policy research and alternatives development. As an NRDC brochure puts it: "The power of law. The power of science. The power of people. In defense of the environment." NRDC's publicity probably peaked with its 1989 battle against Alar, the agricultural chemical used mostly on apples. (Actress Meryl Streep's involvement helped.) But NRDC has been most successful in a lesser-known role: suing environmental violators, including U.S. government agencies. Having won many of its legal battles, NRDC gained the stature to help make it a national player in influencing environmental legislation. Thanks to the efforts of this group, many of these laws still actually have teeth in them.

The Nature Conservancy
1815 North Lynn Street
Arlington, VA 22209
(703) 841-5394

Since 1951 the Nature Conservancy has been one of the foremost groups finding, protecting and maintaining the Earth's rare species and natural communities by preserving the lands they need to survive. Managing some 1,100 preserves valued at nearly $400 million, the Conservancy claims to be protecting 5.5 million acres of land across Canada and the United States. In recent years, the group has initiated several debt-for-nature swaps involving lands in Central and South America. In the U.S., the Conservancy works closely with government agencies and environmental organizations in managing land holdings.

**Sierra Club
P.O. Box 7959
San Francisco,CA 94120
(415) 776-2211**

Founded in 1892 by naturalist John Muir to help preserve the beauty of the Sierra Nevada mountain range, today this is one of the largest and best- known environmental groups. Millions of people have taken advantage of the group's international outdoor expeditions, which operate at all experience levels and go just about everywhere. The Sierra Club has also been instrumental in preserving wilderness areas across the United States, and claims to have helped preserve some 130 million acres of public lands. The Club's books and Sierra journal, in addition to being informative, are always chock-full of absolutely gorgeous photographs.

**The Wilderness Society
900 Seventeenth St., NW
Washington, DC 20006
(202) 833-2300**

Devoted to the preservation of wilderness and wildlife, the Wilderness Society was formed in 1935. Its 350,000 members have helped protect thousands of acres of American wilderness. The group helped push Florida to add 110,000 acres of the East Everglades to the Everglades National Park, and Nevada to set aside 733,400 acres of wilderness in the Humboldt and Toiyabe National Forests. In southeast Alaska, the Society has worked for years to protect the Tongass National Forest, one of the few remaining temperate tropical forests, which is particularly threatened by logging.

**World Wildlife Fund
1250 24th Street, NW
Washington, DC 20037
(202) 293-4800**

WWF is the largest private international nature conservation group, with three million supporters on almost all continents. It seeks to protect the biological resources upon which human well-being depends. Toward this end, WWF has helped establish hundreds of national parks throughout the world in places such as Kenya, Peru and Nepal. Another major WWF program, TRAFFIC, monitors international trade in wild animals and plants with the hope of pressuring governments into curbing this illegal trade.

OUR FAVORITES: NATIONAL ORGANIZATIONS

**American Council for an Energy Efficient Economy
1001 Connecticut Ave., NW
Suite 801
Washington, DC 20036
(202) 429-8873**

One of the premier sources for information regarding energy efficiency, this well recognized non-profit group publishes some excellent (and readable) books and reports relating to energy efficiency. For instance, the *Consumer Guide to Home Energy Savings* details in over 240 pages many practical, easy- to-understand steps that consumers can take to make their homes more energy efficient - and save money in the process. The guide also lists and rates high efficiency appliances and equipment for the home.

**Center for Neighborhood Technology
2125 West North Avenue
Chicago, IL 60647
(312) 278-4800**

The Center for Neighborhood Technology is an environmental research, advocacy and technical assistance organization that provides practical, real- world alternatives to complex local environmental problems. Over the past several years, the Center has developed a healthy, sustainable strategy for the highly toxic metal finishing industry, a critical component of Chicago's economy. Collaboration among metal finishers, regulators, local economic development groups, and the Center produced a waste reduction strategy that is economically feasible for the small firms involved. *Sustainable Manufacturing: Saving Jobs, Saving the Environment* details these and other efforts for concerned citizens to replicate in their own communities and cities.

**Clean Water Action
317 Pennsylvania Ave., SE
Washington, DC 20003
(202) 547-1196**

Focusing on citizen organizing, lobbying and research, Clean Water Action is one of the most active and effective grassroots environmental groups. It was started in 1970 by then-Harvard Law student David Zwick, who had served on a 1968 task force study showing severe drinking and recreational water contamination that the federal government had neither the legal authority nor funding to address. Using citizen campaigns, lobbying, litigation and other means, CWA has successfully challenged unwise development, dangerous industry, and environmental violators across the U.S. CWA's top priorities continue to include drinking water hazards, but have since expanded to cover toxic hazards, coastland and inland waters, and elections. CWA maintains regional and local offices throughout the country.

**Earth Island Institute
300 Broadway, Suite 28
San Francisco, CA 94133
(415) 788-3666**

A major activist environmental group, founded by "archdruid" (in writer John McPhee's words) activist David Brower in 1982 to develop innovative projects for the conservation, preservation and restoration of the global environment. Under Earth Island's nurturing umbrella many successful and well-known organizations got their start, including the Save the Dolphins Project and Rainforest Action Network. Currently some twenty projects are ongoing at Earth Island, ranging from the Sea Turtle Restoration Project to the Environmental Litigation Fund, to the Urban Habitat Program, which acts as a catalyst in developing a multicultural urban environmental leadership. *Earth Island Journal* is a wonderful, low-tech compendium of the most newsworthy environmental stories from around the globe.

**Environmental Protection Agency (EPA)
401 M Street, SW
Washington, DC 20460**

Useful numbers:

• Public Affairs
(202) 382-4361

- Recycled Products Guidelines Hotline (703) 941-4452
- Safe Drinking Water Hotline (800) 426-4791

The EPA offers a long list of publications for nearly every purpose (which is not to say that they're all so wonderful or useful). Parents and teachers can call the Office of Public Affairs for lesson plans and materials about recycling or pollution prevention, a list of *Books for Young People on Environmental Issues*, and much more. Keep in mind that the EPA goes out of its way to avoid controversy, and at least one of its recent publications for consumers have been withdrawn due to industry pressure (for instance, some companies didn't like the fact that the EPA suggested that bringing your own mug to work could be more environmentally friendly than using disposable cups!).

**Friends of the Earth
218 D Street, SE
Washington, DC 20003
(202) 544-2600**

Founded in 1969 by David Brower, FOE merged in 1990 with Environmental Policy Institute and the Oceanic Society. Friends of the Earth International has affiliates in many countries throughout the world's continents, including Israel. Perhaps best known for its gutsy grassroots actions and protests (it stopped a billion-dollar subsidy to the Synthetic Fuels Corporation and successfully opposed the construction of several nuclear power plants), it has increasingly been producing critical studies of corporate environmental misdeeds, among other things.

**Green Seal
1733 Connecticut Ave., NW
Washington, DC 20009
(202) 328-8095**

Available soon near you: Eco-labeling on products like writing paper, light bulbs, and others. The Green Seal will be awarded to those products least harmful to the environment, for instance the writing paper with the highest amount of post-consumer recycled content and no chlorine bleaching. It is modelled on the highly successful Blue Angel program operating in Germany since 1975.

**Institute for Local Self-Reliance
2425 18th Street, NW
Washington, DC 20009
(202) 232-4108**

This immensely successful group provides practical solutions for communities and municipalities seeking to address their solid waste problems. Staunch supporters of community recycling, the Institute's publication, *Beyond 40 Percent*, documents municipal recycling programs across the United States that have succeeded in surpassing a 40% participation rate.

**International Rivers Network
1847 Berkeley Way
Berkeley, CA 94703
(510) 848-1155**

As a direct consequence of the reckless damming, channeling and polluting of waterways millions of people are forcibly displaced, productive farmland is lost, river fisheries, wetlands and estuaries are destroyed, and irreversible damage is wreaked on the world's rivers. International Rivers Network is a super effective international organization dedicated to fighting this "development." Its

members include environmentalists, engineers, hydrologists, human rights activists and academics. IRN's network of citizens groups spans over 80 countries. Because many large-scale hydroelectric projects (dams) are sponsored by the World Bank, the group also focuses efforts on criticizing and protesting bank policies and plans.

**The Joint Appeal by Religion and Science for the Environment
Cathedral of Saint John the Divine
(212) 316-7441
(800) 826-9800**

Believing that the environment is "an inescapably religious challenge," this group brings together religious and scientific leaders committed to the environmental cause. The toll-free number allows congregations of all denominations to share news of their environmental activities, which as this book shows, can range from "adopting" a local stream to installing a solar-powered eternal light. One project of the Joint Appeal is the Consultation on the Environment and Jewish Life, a broad-based, non-denominational coalition of Jewish leaders and rabbis seeking to help environmental issues infiltrate Jewish communal and personal life.

**The Land Institute
2440 E. Water Well Rd.
Salina, KS 63401
(913) 823-5376**

Founded by agricultural and nature preservation iconoclast Wes Jackson, The Land Institute is the breeding ground for experimental work in ecosystem-level agriculture. On more than 200 acres, scientists and

interns representing the fields of genetics, ecology, entomology, plant pathology and the humanities seek a sustainable agriculture that fits in with its natural surroundings, in this case the native American prairie.

**Local Solutions to Global Pollution
2121 Bonar, Studio A
Berkeley, CA 94702
(510) 540-8843**

An outgrowth of Berkeley City Councilmember Nancy Skinner's work on innovative environmental policies specifically related to solid waste source reduction efforts, bans of ozone-depleting compounds/processes, and reductions of greenhouse gas emissions. Local Solutions' philosophy is to approach environmental problems through pollution prevention rather than control. Materials and publications are sold which are applicable to local actions and efforts.

**The National Arbor Day Foundation
100 Arbor Avenue
Nebraska City, NE 68410
(402) 474-5655**

Springing from the national holiday, this group encourages individuals and organizations to help further the cause of conservation and tree planting all year round. *The Conservation Trees* booklet, distributed to over 1.3 million Americans already, teaches how to use trees for windbreaks and energy conservation, how to prune trees, and more. The Trees for America program has given out over 7 million trees and one million copies of *The Tree Book*, which also provides tree planting and care information. The program hopes to have every citizen plant a tree.

Native Seeds/SEARCH
3950 West New York Drive
Tucson, AZ 85745
(602) 327-9123

Founded by ethnobotanist Gary Paul Nabhan, Native Seeds/Search conserves traditional crop seeds and other wild seeds of the American Southwest.

New Alchemy Institute
237 Hatchville Road East
Falmouth, MA 02536
(508) 564-6301

Founded in 1969 as a research and education center, it has been described as the grand-daddy of integrated/demonstration farms. Located on 12 acres in Cape Cod, the Institute is a living laboratory of more sustainable farming. The New Alchemists, as they call themselves, are just that. They have, for example, grown papayas in solar-heated greenhouses. Their "ark" houses multi-levels of plants, fish, water plants, and helpful insects — heated partially from underneath by compost bins. The Institute has an extensive children's program, and classes in organic gardening and nature studies are available in the summer. Fall programs are designed for children and their parents, and a school program is available throughout the school year. The Institute offers a training manual for teachers, and teacher workshops at school or at the institute.

North American Permaculture
P.O. Box 573
Colville, WA 99114

Agricultural activist Bill Mollison coined the term "permaculture" (permanent agriculture) in the late 1970s, meaning the conscious design and maintenance of economically and agriculturally productive ecosystems that have the diversity, stability and resilience of natural ecosystems. While focusing on agricultural systems, however, permaculture also establishes the importance of integration between landscape and people. Several books and a quarterly journal devoted to permaculture provide abundant conceptual and hands-on help. There are actually many permaculture groups in the United States, and even more internationally. North American Permaculture is a good place to get started, though, and will refer you to local groups near you.

Pesticide Action Network
Box 610
San Francisco, CA 94101
(415) 541-9140

An international network of people and groups campaigning to end agriculture's over-reliance on toxic chemicals, Pesticide Action Network is known for its thorough research and effective protests. For information on the impact of any agricultural chemical, this is the place to go. PAN's database of international activists can also hook you up with potential allies abroad, from South America to South Africa.

Rainforest Action Network
301 Broadway, Suite A
San Francisco, CA 94133
(415) 398-4404

This international network of activists fighting to protect Earth's rainforests was founded in 1985 by Randy Hayes. It rocketed to prominence (and success) through its 1987 Burger King protest campaign and boycott. In response to RAN's efforts, Burger King cancelled $35 million worth of Central American beef contracts. The campaign also helped thrust rainforest issues into public consciousness. Currently, some 150 Rainforest Action Groups operate under the RAN umbrella across the United States. In addition, RAN works closely with indigenous activists in South American, East Asian and tropical Pacific countries in seeking to ban tropical timber exports (imports, depending on where you live).

Renew America
1400 16th Street, NW
Suite 710
Washington, DC 20036
(202) 232-2252

Looking for a successful way to fight local air pollution? Interested in how other communities are achieving recycling goals? Contact Renew America, a clearinghouse for environmental solutions. Renew America runs the Searching for Success awards, which seek out the best and most creative solutions to specific, local problems. *The Environmental Success Index* lists some 1500 of these model projects, and will save you great a amount of time and energy in your own research. Renew America's *State of the States* annual report card documents how each state ranks according to environmental conditions, including air pollution, groundwater contamination, environmental laws, and more.

Restoring the Earth
1713C Martin Luther King Jr. Way
Berkeley, CA 94709

Founded in 1985 to focus attention on creative solutions to environmental problems by means of ecological restoration.

Rocky Mountain Institute
1739 Snowmass Creek Rd.
Snowmass, CO 81654
(303) 927-3851

The place to go for information on energy efficiency. Founded and run by energy efficiency guru Amory Lovins and his wife Hunter Lovins, Rocky Mountain Institute seeks workable alternatives for homes, offices and factories. The Institute's offices are housed in a model home, whose design, materials, low-emissivity windows and computer-operated heating/cooling system make it so energy efficient that Rocky Mountain Institute actually sells power back to the local electric utility! The ideas developed through the Institute's research are promoted in books, catalogs of available products, and through the Competitek consulting division, which works with business clients in the U.S. and abroad.

Rodale Institute and Press
222 Main Street
Emmaus, PA 18098
(215) 967-5171

Rodale seeks to advance the public well-being in the areas of food, health and natural resources. It publishes *The New Farm*, *Organic Gardening* and *Prevention* magazines, as well as a host of other important books on organic gardening and agriculture. Rodale's philosophy of gardening and farming is tried out on the 305-acre Rodale Research Center, where the efforts are geared mostly toward the needs of the home gardener and small-scale farmer. An annual day-long GardenFest allows people to come sample the fruits (literally) of the research.

Seeds of Change
621 Old Santa Fe Trail #10
Santa Fe, NM 87501
(505) 983-8956

Distributors of organic seeds, protectors of native American seed varieties, the people at Seeds of Change also produce what is perhaps the most wonderful, colorful and informative seed catalog you'll ever read.

Seventh Generation
Department 60M89
10 Farrell Street
Burlington, VT 05403
(800) 456-1177

Environmentally-sound mail-order catalog. Seventh Generation sells everything from solar-powered accessories to non-toxic cleaners and recycled paper products.

Whole Earth Catalog
Portola Institute
Menlo Park, CA 94025
(415) 845-3000

While not an environmental organization per se, the *Whole Earth Catalogs* and the quarterly *Whole Earth Review* offer a host of alternative products, books and ways of thinking. Founder Stewart Brand has forged for Whole Earth an eclectic style of approaching environmental and other issues, one that in a sense has come to define a certain "new age" outlook, willing to meld electronic communication with "primitive" diet, twentieth-century critical analysis with traditional spiritualities.

World Resources Institute
1735 New York Ave., NW
Washington, DC 20006
(202) 638-6300

This policy research center tackles major questions of environmental protection and industrial growth. WRI publishes an exceptionally informative and visually pleasing annual report, *World Resources*, on the state of the world's environmental health that has become a standard reference volume.

Worldwatch Institute
1776 Massachusetts Avenue, NW
Washington, DC 20036
(202) 452-1999

Founded in 1975 and run by agricultural expert and activist Lester Brown, this influential environmental think tank has redefined the shape of the movement. Its major goal is to inform the public and the policy-makers about the relationship between economic and environmental issues — and they are succeeding. Worldwatch's excellent journal, *Worldwatch*, its many papers and reports, and its annual *State of the World* book are premier sources of current information. *State of the World* is translated into more than 10 languages, an indication of its importance.

LOCAL ORGANIZATIONS

BOSTON

Citizen's Energy Corporation
530 Atlantic Avenue
Boston, MA 02210
(617) 951-0400

Includes the Walden Pond Project, which is trying to raise money *to purchase* Walden Pond in order to protect it from the imminent threat of local developers (irony of ironies).

CHICAGO

Citizens for a Better Environment
407 S. Dearborn
Suite 1775
Chicago, Il 60605
(312) 939-1350

This group of activists and lobbyists fights to reduce toxic pollution and make Chicago's workplaces and neighborhoods safe and healthy.

Lake Michigan Federation
59 East Van Buren
Suite 2215
Chicago, IL 60605
(312) 939-0838

Four-state coalition of citizens for the protection of Lake Michigan.

CONNECTICUT

Sounds Conservancy
P.O. Box 266
43 Main Street
Essex, CT 06426
(203) 767-1933

Conserves, restores and protects the marine region of Long Island, Block Island, Fishers Island, Rhode Island, Martha's Vineyard and Nantucket Sounds.

HOUSTON

Texans United
3400 Montrose Avenue
Suite 225
Houston, TX 77006
(713) 453-0853

Since 1989, Texans United has worked to build a strong citizens' movement in Texas — one which protects the environment without sacrificing jobs. Texans United is affiliated with the National Toxics Campaign, a nationwide coalition working to implement solutions to the nation's toxic and environmental problems. Texans United works on fighting toxic hazards and petrochemical pollution (a major local problem), and works on farm issues and electoral environmental issues.

LOS ANGELES

Community Environmental Council Gildea Resource Center
930 Miramonte Drive
Santa Barbara, CA 93109
(805) 963-0583

Although primarily a local group, the influence of the Community Environmental Council emanates around the country. The group's excellent research studies on issues such as recycling and sustainable economics have long been read by environmentalists everywhere. At home in Santa Barbara, CEC offers curbside recycling throughout California's South Coast, hazardous waste collection days, and maintenance of three public gardens where people are welcome to come and grow their own food. CEC advises local governments and businesses on recycling and participates in keeping the local environmental planning process on-track and in the best interests of local people and resources.

Heal the Bay
1650A 10th Street
Santa Monica, CA 90404
(213) 399-1146

Dedicated to restoring the Santa Monica Bay.

Labor/Community Strategy Center
14540 Haynes Street
Suite 200
Van Nuys, CA 91411
(818) 781-4800

The Labor/Community Strategy Center is a multi-racial center for policy, strategy and organizing in Los Angeles. Its emphasis is unabashedly progressive. With the involvement of several labor unions, neighborhood groups and social justice organizations, the Center's environmental arm, the Labor/Community Watchdog, fights for clean air in L.A. Realizing that poor and minority communities bear the largest burden of pollution, the Labor/Community Strategy Center pressures politicians for affordable mass transit and clean, unionized industry. As the Center sees it, "the environmental crisis, and its resolution, hinges on production and who controls it."

TreePeople
12601 Mulholland Drive
Beverly Hills, CA 90210
(213) 753-4600

MIAMI

Friends of the Everglades
202 Park Street
Miami, FL 33166
(305) 888-1230

Friends of the Everglades works to foster and facilitate through education a harmonious co-existence between human and natural environmental systems in the Everglades.

NEW YORK

Council on the Environment of New York City
51 Chambers Street, Room 228
New York, NY 10007
(212) 566-0990

Since 1976, this wonderfully effective group has operated New York's outstanding 26 Greenmarkets, bringing together small regional farmers with urban consumers (in 1991 it won the national Rudy Bruner Award for Excellence in the Urban Environment). CENYC's Open Space Greening Program has assisted hundreds of community garden projects with technical and material assistance. Both of these programs are unique in serving traditionally under-served sections of the city, such as Harlem, Brownsville, Bedford-Stuyvesant and the Bronx, as well as many other New York neighborhoods. The Office Paper Recycling Service Plus designs and installs cost-effective recycling programs and recommends other ways for office buildings to "reduce, reuse and recycle." The Training Student Organizers Program works in high schools and colleges, where it teaches students to organize environmental improvement projects in their communities.

Environmental Action Coalition
625 Broadway
New York, NY 10012
(212) 677-1601

Starting small in 1970, the Environmental Action Coalition has grown to become a New York fixture. The group works to solve New York's environmental problems at the local level. Efforts focus on source-separation recycling, monitoring resource recovery installations, urban reforestation and environmental education projects.

NYC Street Tree Consortium
(212) 227-1887

Want to lend a hand to local street trees? This is the place to get involved, get trained and get active. Citizen volunteers learn to maintain New York's street trees by pruning branches, cultivating soil in tree pits, removing guy wires that impede growth and identifying pest problems. Citizen Street Tree Pruners are certified by the Parks Department, and over 2200 people have taken the required coursework offered by the Consortium.

Operation GreenThumb Department of General Services
49 Chambers Street, Room 1020
New York, NY 10007
(212) 233-2926

Operation Green Thumb, NYC Department of General Services' community gardening program, leases city-owned vacant lots for $1.00 a year to non- profit community organizations so they can establish neighborhood-sponsored gardens. Hundreds of GreenThumb gardens — in all shapes and sizes — flourish throughout the city, providing an estimated $1,000,000 worth of fruits and vegetables annually (not to mention the incalculable joy and benefits they bring). Training workshops are provided to the sponsoring organizations, as well as materials, tools, lumber, soil, etc.

Terra Verde
72 Spring Street
New York, NY
(212) 925-4533

Great, green store for natural, alternative and environmentally-sound products. Terra Verde opened in New York in 1990 and in Santa Monica in October 1991 (see under Los Angeles). Metropolitan Home called Terra Verde "the best — and first — ecological department store," "practical and poetic." Stop in to shop, or just to read up on the literature the store makes available to customers.

Transportation Alternatives
P.O. Box 2087
New York, NY 10009
(212) 334-9343

This somewhat off-the-beaten-track organization (pun intended) is made up of bicycle commuters, environmentalists and others who support responsible and sane alternatives to private car proliferation.

PHILADELPHIA

Pennsylvania Resources Council
P.O. Box 88
Media, PA 19063
(215) 565-9131

Pennsylvania Resources Council works on recycling and solid waste issues. PRC encourages environmentally-responsible shopping, and provides members with Environmental Shopping kits (one for kids, one for adults). Along these lines, PRC has been very active in the debate about environmental labeling for products, and in sponsoring and organizing an annual Environmental Shopping Conference. PRC also produces a long list of easy-to-understand publications on the above and other topics, useful for schools, businesses or community groups.

Philadelphia Greens/Pennsylvania Horticultural Society
325 Walnut Street
Philadelphia, PA 19106
(215) 625-8280

Schuykill Valley Nature Center
8480 Hagy's Mill Road
Philadelphia, PA 19128
(215) 482-7300

SAN FRANCISCO

Abalone Alliance
2940 16th Street, #310
San Francisco, CA 94103
(415) 861-0592

Formed in 1977 by activists, Quakers and "anarcha-feminists" across California to protest the construction and operation of the Diablo Canyon nuclear power plant near San Luis Obispo, Abalone Alliance has since continued to fight, in California and nationwide, for a sane, safe energy policy. Barbara Epstein, in her excellent new book, *Political Protest and Cultural Revolution: Nonviolent Direct Action in the 1970s and 1980s*, writes that "The Abalone's most important contribution to the direct action movement was the internal culture it created — a commitment to nonviolence combined with a utopian vision of a radically democratic society..."

BayKeeper, a project of the San Francisco Bay - Delta Preservation Association
Building A, Fort Mason
San Francisco, CA 94123
(415) 567-4401

Modelled on New York's Hudson RiverKeeper program, BayKeeper uses volunteers to patrol the San Francisco Bay and its shorelines on foot, via aircraft, and by boat to detect violations of environmental laws. During its short lifespan, BayKeeper has been enormously successful in monitoring water quality and reporting pollution incidents, advocating and initiating litigation against violators, and serving as an antenna for citizen complaints. BayKeeper also creates an informed voting constituency which is aware of both the Bay's unique bio/ecological value and current threats to its health.

East Bay Citizens for Creek Restoration
2721 Stuart Street
Berkeley, CA 94705
(510) 486-1742

Ecology Center
2530 San Pablo Avenue
Berkeley, CA 94702
(510) 548-2220

Serving the area since 1969, the Ecology Center has grown to the point where it now operates Berkeley's curbside recycling program and two weekly farmers' markets! This is on top of the excellent environmental library and information service, organic gardening supply center and organic gardening classes, bookstore and monthly newsletter.

Greenbelt Alliance
116 New Montgomery St.
Suite 640
San Francisco, CA 94105
(415) 543-4291

Since 1958, Greenbelt Alliance has fought to protect the Bay Area's Greenbelt of open lands — and it has become a force to be reckoned with. The Alliance helped save Napa vineyards, Angel Island, South Bay farmlands, and parklands in the East Bay and Sonoma County — more than 500,000 acres in the last decade alone. The Alliance also produces significant, original research that shows how to balance housing, jobs and transportation needs with protecting farmlands and other productive open lands.

Merritt College - Self-Reliant House Environmental Education Center
12500 Campus Drive
Oakland, CA 94619
(510) 436-2619

Offers broad-based environmental education for a community college. In particular, people with skills are sought for help in completing this model environmental house. Contact: Mr. Robin Freeman (510) 848-5713.

San Francisco Friends of the Urban Forest
512 2nd Street, 4th Floor
San Francisco, CA 94107
(415) 543-5000

Uses city trees to provide an exciting laboratory in which students can explore their physical environment and community from many perspectives. *City Trees: A Curriculum Guide of Our Urban Forest and Community*. Free walking tours. Tree planting.

San Francisco League of Urban Gardeners
2540 Newhall Street
San Francisco, CA 94124
(415) 285-7584

How can you resist a group with the acronym SLUG? Well over 70 community and school gardens around San Francisco couldn't. SLUG operates a senior center rooftop garden and a handicap-accessible garden, helps acquire vacant city lots to preserve as gardening space, involves hundreds of schoolkids every year in learning programs, and even teaches adults how to improve or acquire green thumbs. SLUG is as well-loved around the Bay Area as its namesake is hated.

Slide Ranch
2025 Shoreline Hwy.
Muir Beach, CA 94965
(415) 381-6155

A non-profit demonstration farm and environmental education center operating as a park partner with the Golden Gate National Recreation Area, Slide Ranch has been offering educational programs since 1970 to school children, the learning and physically disadvantaged, inner-city kids, multi-ethnic groups, Girl and Boy Scouts, and other organizations. Kids might dig compost into a garden bed, plant seeds, milk goats, or spin sheeps' wool. Slide Ranch also offers family days and internship programs.

Sonoma Energy Extension Center c/o Sonoma State University Department of Environmental Studies
Rohnert Park, CA 94928
(707) 664-3145

Part of a nationwide effort to lower energy use for small-scale consumers, the California Energy Extension Service operates many demonstration projects, including schools. Regional energy extension centers strive to make participating schools as energy efficient as possible with the involvement of everybody at the school.

Urban Ecology
P.O. Box 10144
Berkeley, CA 94709
(510) 549-1724

Working toward ecologically, economically and socially sustainable urban environments, Urban Ecology is an international network of experts and activists. The focus is on design/planning, transportation, energy, and physical environment issues.

WASHINGTON, DC

Alliance for the Chesapeake Bay
660 York Road
Baltimore, MD 21212
(800) 662-CRIS

This federation of citizens' organizations, business enterprises and scientists has worked since 1971 to preserve the Chesapeake Bay. The Alliance hosts conferences, sponsors field trips, organizes citizen volunteers, supports grassroots conservation activities and organizations, and offers a toll-free information service to local residents.

Center for Urban Ecology Jobs in Energy 1120 Riverside Avenue Baltimore, MD 21230 (301) 659-0683

A coalition of local civil rights, religious, labor, environmental and community groups that establishes and operates energy conservation projects which create jobs.

ISRAEL:

Hai-Bar Society for the Establishment of Biblical National Wildlife Reserves
c/o Nature Reserves Authority
78 Yirmeyahu Street
Jerusalem 94467 ISRAEL

Working to establish reserves in Israel for animals mentioned in the Bible, this group has already set up several such wildlife sanctuaries. A great deal of research is done at these locations. Visitors are encouraged to visit.

Haifa Environmental Action Committee

Haifa's industrial air pollution problems are legion, by far the worst in Israel. This group organized several years ago to fight for cleaner air, beginning with 30 mostly American and Canadian citizens living in Israel. By 1990, the group's numbers reached some 800, mostly native Israelis. One of the organization's many successes was gathering 30,000 signatures in 1988 to prevent the building of yet another power plant in Haifa. Since then it has campaigned to pressure politicians to improve the city's air quality.

Israel Agency for Nuclear Information

Established in 1986 by former American activist Shirley Benjamin, this grass-roots organization succeeded in setting up the first Israeli library of nuclear information. It is located at the Hebrew University Hadassah Medical School in Jerusalem.

Neot Kidumim
Society for the Protection of Nature in Israel
Main Office 3 Hashfela St.
Tel Aviv 66183 ISRAEL

American Society for the Protection of Nature in Israel
330 Seventh Avenue
21st Floor
New York, NY 10001
(212) 947-2820

From its beginnings in 1953, the SPNI and its American counterpart (formed to increase support among American Jews) have had as its aim to teach respect, understanding and love of nature and the land. As Israel's largest independent membership organization, the SPNI involves nearly 20% of the Israeli population (including Muslims and Christians) in outdoor recreational and educational activities; operates a network of 25 field study centers; develops conservation strategies together with Israeli universities; stimulates environmental awareness in development towns and disadvantaged urban areas; conducts nature tours; and much more.

ENVIRONMENTAL EDUCATION

Audubon Canyon Ranch
4900 Shoreline Highway, Rt. 1
Stinson Beach, CA 94970
(415) 868-9244

Some 6,000 San Francisco Bay Area kids a year have the opportunity to face a western fence lizard, discover what lives in a pond or watch spectacular herons. One-day field trips visit one of three beautiful local nature preserves accompanied by a one-day in-school seminar (for 3rd through 6th graders only).

California Marine Mammal Center
Marin Headlands Golden Gate National Recreation Area
Sausalito, CA 94965
(415) 289-SEAL

Located on an abandoned Nike missile base, CMMC has rescued and rehabilitated hundreds of marine mammals of all kinds since its founding in 1975. CMMC has an active education department that works to make the public more aware of the ocean's ecosystem and the marine environment and provides an up-close look at CMMC's operations. Groups of up to 35 can visit for $40, with tours geared for the group's level. Its hands-on programs provide excellent training for school children.

Environmental Traveling Companions (ETC)
Fort Mason Center, Building C
San Francisco, CA 94123
(415) 474-7662

"Adventures that make a difference" says ETC, and they're not kidding! Since 1971, ETC has been helping those who might not otherwise get outdoors get way outdoors, and learn a lot about themselves as they do. Three programs (river rafting, sea kayaking, and winter trips) allow those with special needs, including youth-at-risk, students, and people who are visually or hearing impaired, physically or developmentally disabled, and those with a terminal illness such as AIDS, to challenge themselves in unique, guided situations.

Global Warming:
Understanding the Forecast
A Travelling Exhibit

American Museum of Natural History, New York -through January 19, 1993
Check with your local museum to find out when this exhibit will visit you.

Co-produced by the Environmental Defense Fund, this elaborate and high-tech exhibit allows viewers access to understanding a wide range of global warming issues. Interactive computer panels explain the debate about the planet's heating up due to rising carbon dioxide (and other gases). A model cow with a neon gut and burping loudspeaker is a visceral reminder of the contribution of cattle to the release of methane (another dangerous gas) into the atmosphere. Real Greenland ice (behind a window) clouded with 660-year- old air bubbles helps show how scientists use ice core samples to study the composition of air in past epochs. Well thought-out, and allowing for dissenting opinions, the global warming exhibit stands as a model of environmental education for all age groups — filled with scientific explanations, and conveying concern for the fate of our planet, without being preachy.

Life Lab Science Program
1156 High Street
Santa Cruz, CA 95060
(408) 459-2001

This kindergarten to sixth grade, garden-based science program is used by schools across the country to encourage kids to learn by growing their own plants. Community support and participation is highly encouraged. Two-day training workshops for teachers can be arranged and curriculum can be obtained through the program office. Life Lab has won four awards over its ten- year lifespan.

**Melton Center
Jewish Theological Seminary
of America
3080 Broadway
New York, NY 10027
(212) 678-8996**

Founded in 1960, the Seminary's Melton Center is dedicated to research in and service to Jewish education. Two issues of the Center's *Melton Journal* (Spring 1991 and Spring 1992) have focused on Jewish ecological themes, and are replete with thoughtful and useful essays by a wide variety of Jewish leaders and thinkers.

**Project Learning Tree
1250 Connecticut Ave., NW
Suite 320-FG
Washington, DC 20036
(202) 463-2468**

Award-winning interdisciplinary environmental education program designed for teachers and other educators working with students in K - 12. Using the forest as a "window" into the natural world, Project Learning Tree helps young people become aware of the natural world around them, and their place within it. With PLT materials, classes can adopt a tree, go on a school safari, discover the secret ingredients in soil, or test the effects of overcrowding on plant growth. Workshops and other teacher training classes are offered throughout the United States.

**Project WILD
P.O. Box 18060
Boulder, CO 80308
(303) 444-2390**

A nationwide program for K - 12 teachers, Project WILD is sponsored by public agencies in each state. Using a multidisciplinary approach, the program teaches teachers and children about wildlife concepts, and provides workshops and educational materials to assist in this effort. Over 20 million students have already benefited from this wonderful program. Project WILD received a Special Merit citation from Renew America's *Searching for Success* environmental achievement program.

**The Urban Tree House/
Sussman Environmental
Center Children's Museum
of Manhattan
212 West 83rd Street
New York, NY 10025
(212) 721-1234**

Featuring hands-on exhibits for kids on the theme "reduce, recycle, re-use and rethink," this new museum is the perfect place for kids (and their adults) to learn about environmental protection while having loads of fun. Where else can you watch a composting bin "in action," with 4,000 earthworms doing their dirty but essential work?

**Wildlife Inquiry through Zoo
Education (WIZE)
Annette Berkovits Curator
of Education and Director of
Project WIZE
Bronx Zoo New York
Zoological Society
185th Street and Southern
Boulevard
Bronx, NY 10460
(212) 220-5135 or
220-6855**

Using a non-traditional, multi-disciplinary approach (including suggested visits to zoos and other natural history institutions), the WIZE program improves understanding of concepts related to population, ecology, wildlife conservation, and species survival. Students work toward solutions which cause the least disruption to the environmen. Teacher training is available. Appropriate for students in grades 7 - 9.

MEDIA

**Bullfrog Films
Oley, PA 19547
(800) 543-3764**

Rents and sells films to educational institutions.

**Environmental Film Review
Environment Information
Center
Film Reference Department
292 Madison Avenue
New York, NY 10017**

Films and catalog available.

**Environmental Film Service
National Association of
Conservation Districts
408 East Main
P.O. Box 855
League City, TX 77573
(713) 332-3402**

Makes available to the public films on the environment and conservation.

**Environmental Images, Inc.
300 I Street, NW
Suites 100 & 325
Washington, DC 20036
(202) 675-9100**

Films, videotapes, and slides available.

**Media Network
39 West 14th Street
Suite 403
New York, NY 10011
(212) 929-2663**

Media Network is a national membership organization helping concerned individuals use video for social change. Produces *Safe Planet: The Guide to Environmental Film and Video*, containing over 60 titles addressing environmental issues and grassroots activism.

There are just so many excellent and important books dealing with environmental issues that any list such as this will necessarily be quite selective. We divided our choices into two categories: nature writing and environmental politics. Obviously, many titles fit into both, and even the categorization itself is somewhat arbitrary.

NATURE WRITING

Wendell Berry; *Continuous Harmony*; Harcourt Brace Jovanovich, 1970. *The Gift of Good Land*; North Point Press, 1981. *Home Economics. The Unsettling of America: Culture and Agriculture*; 1977.

A poet and farmer himself, Berry continually returns to the theme of proper relationship to the land, to our environment. He celebrates respectful, joyful work, while also respecting wilderness and its refusal to be worked. In all his writings, his language startles with its beauty and clarity. His is a prophetic voice, one born of the American soil.

Annie Dillard; *Pilgrim at Tinker Creek*; Harper and Row, 1974. *Teaching a Stone to Talk: Expeditions and Encounters*; Harper and Row, 1982.

Annie Dillard's profoundly beautiful books have become the model for contemporary American nature writing. Not simply a description of nature's ways, Dillard's writing hovers over the face of nature's chaos, it probes nature's cruelty and beauty, it explores our own feelings in the presence of all this and more. We are inseparable from this absurd and sublime universe, and in a personal yet mythopoetic way, Dillard's writing attempts to understand us and nature — not to answer the questions posed by the inseparability, but to let the very questions resonate.

Loren Eisley; *The Immense Journey*; Random House, 1957. *The Unexpected Universe*; Harcourt Brace Jovanovich, 1964.

Anthropologist and naturalist, Loren Eisley has written some of the most influential books on humans and nature. Profoundly personal, his meditations on our history and situation are pervaded by a brooding sense of how we stand apart, somewhat alone from our surroundings. At the same time, there is perhaps no other writer who so well captures how much an animal we remain, a fact that inspires in him some consolation for the burdens of our consciousness.

Vicki Hearne; *Adam's Task: Calling Animals by Name*; Vintage Books, 1987.

This unique, provocative, warm and very funny book by Vicki Hearne, a poet, assistant professor of English at Yale and professional horse and dog trainer, is about how we relate to our domestic animals (and vice versa). More accurately, perhaps, it teaches important and illuminating lessons — without ideological hang-ups — about how people who own or work with animals must earn the right to "command" them within a reciprocal relationship.

Aldo Leopold; *A Sand County Almanac*; Ballantine, 1989.

First printed in 1949, shortly after Leopold had died fighting a fire, this short journal of a year in rural Wisconsin is a model of nature observation, a classic for conservation ethics. Stylistically, *A Sand County Almanac* contains both magnificent attentiveness to nature's smallest cycles and beings as well as thoughtful excursions into the philosophy of nature, what Leopold calls "the ecological conscience." Leopold, who taught wildlife management at the University of Wisconsin, here celebrates the quietude of nature, but he is already aware of the degradation and impoverishment that has begun to creep over nature.

James Lovelock; *Gaia: A New Look at Life on Earth*; Oxford University Press, 1979.

James Lovelock, an independent scientist who worked on, among other things, the NASA space effort, first proposed his Gaia hypothesis — that the earth is a single living organism — in the mid-1960's. Lovelock argues that the earth's living mater — air, ocean and land surfaces — forms a complex system which has the capacity to keep our planet a fit place for life. Although on first publication most of the scientific establishment refused to even discuss its eccentric conclusions (from their point of view), much of the hypothesis has since been corroborated by scientific research. A somewhat difficult book, with enough technical material to daunt the layperson, it is nonetheless wonderful reading, sensitive, thoughtful, at times poetic. This is scientific writing at its best.

Malcolm Margolin; *The Ohlone Way*; Heyday Books, 1978.

A Boston-born Jew transplanted to California, Malcolm Margolin has devoted his life to the understanding of Native American cultures. This book is a remarkably sensitive, moving and evocative portrait of the way the pre-European residents of the San Francisco Bay Area lived. Among other things, it teaches that their enemies (who saw them as primitives living in the wilderness) and those who romanticize their "wild and free" ways were and are both wrong. They lived, instead, in a delicate balance within an ecosystem which they wisely and sustainably cultivated.

Gary Paul Nabhan; *Enduring Seeds. Gathering the Desert. The Desert Smells Like Rain*; North Point Press, 1987.

Gary Paul Nabhan, pioneer and saint of seed protection, is an ethnobotanist by training. His writing is intensely personal, even while it transcends its subject — usually the plant wisdom of southwest native peoples — to become something like a metaphysics of plants and their ecosystems (which have included us for the past seven to ten thousand years). You will learn about the past, present and future of our foods, plants and agriculture from Gary Paul Nabhan's books. And the process will be as enjoyable as eating, which will itself be transformed for you by the new knowledge he shares.

Robert Finch and John Elder, eds; *The Norton Book of Nature Writing*; W.W. Norton and Co., 1990.

A testament to the power of the human encounter with nature, this excellent compendium is both thorough and eclectic. Including 125 selections from 94 writers since the 18th century, this is the most comprehensive anthology of nature writing in the English language ever produced. From Darwin's ruminations on the Galapagos Islands, Melville's explorations of the "whiteness of the whale" and John Muir's first glimpse of the Sierra Nevada's "Range of Light" to Edward Hoagland's verbal capture of the elusive mountain lion, Thomas Merton's brilliant discourse on rain and existential rhinoceri and Ursula Le Guin's interpretation of the mythmaking that surrounded the eruption of Mount St. Helens — this book has everything a reader interested in nature could desire.

Alan Rabinowitz; *Jaguar: One Man's Struggle to Save Jaguars in the Wild*; William Collins, 1987.

A young naturalist fresh out of graduate school, Alan Rabinowitz goes to Belize to study the threatened local jaguar population in the hopes of establishing the world's first jaguar preserve. The locals, not overly fond of jaguars to begin with, find this strange American's quest to protect these misunderstood predators even stranger. This very intense and personal story, could be read as the trials and tribulations of any naturalist working in the field who loves his animal subjects but knows he will always be an outsider. The relationships he forms with both the jaguars and the locals are fraught with complexities, all of which are movingly rendered.

Lewis Thomas; *The Lives of a Cell: Notes of a Biology Watcher*; Viking, 1974. *The Medusa and the Snail: More Notes of a Biology Watcher*; Viking, 1979.

Filled with startling observations, innovative discussions of cellular biology, sharp wit and sensitive yet unsentimental portraits of ecological issues, Lewis Thomas' writings are well-known and well-loved. Thomas is able to make complex, sophisticated concepts easy to grasp. He is also an advocate for nature's resilience and toughness, which in his view comes from the fact that our planetary ecosystem is possibly the universe's largest single natural membrane — intelligent, coping and provident.

Henry David Thoreau; *The Portable Thoreau*; Viking Penguin, 1982.

This anthology of Thoreau's writing has been reprinted over and over since it first appeared in 1947. It contains much of Thoreau's nature-related pieces: *Walden*, excerpts from *The Natural History of Massachusetts*, *A Winter Walk*, *The Maine Woods*, *A Week on the Concord and Merrimack*, *Walking*, poems, several letters, journal entries, and much more. Walden has long been a classic of American naturalism. From the shores of the same-named lake Thoreau gazes at nature, man and society, evaluating what he sees. Thoreau was typically American in his unwillingness to be pigeonholed, to adhere to the "rules" of life. His writings range from depictions of the microcosm, the personal and the intimate to stabs at capturing the wilderness which transcends human understanding. His experimental, playful and often self-conscious style is a wonder to read a century and a half later, remarkable for its prescience as well as its sheer elegance.

Herman J. Viola, Carolyn Margolis, ed.; *Seeds of Change: Five Hundred Years Since Columbus*; Smithsonian Institution Press, 1991.

In this, the quincentenary of Columbus' stumbling onto the New World, one appropriate avenue for exploring ecological issues is a look at the radical environmental changes brought about by the meeting of the Old and New Worlds. This bountifully illustrated collection of essays by eminent scholars of botany, geography, environmental history and other fields provides a wonderful glimpse into that irrevocable transformation of our planet. For instance, before 1492, sugarcane and coffee were unknown in the Americas and potatoes, corn and tomatoes were foreign to Europe. Neither smallpox nor measles existed in the New World before the arrival of Europeans, nor did horses or cattle yet roam the plains and pampas. Hard to imagine!

David Rains Wallace; *The Klamath Knot*; Sierra Club Books, 1983.

In this John Burroughs Medal-winning book, David Rains Wallace uses the Klamath mountain wilderness of the Pacific northwest as a mirror with which to reflect on evolution, "the great myth of modern times." Wallace's elegant writing easily weaves an articulate web from strands as diverse as the "Bigfoot" legends, medieval alchemy, the (mis)applications of evolutionary theory, and more. Finding that humans are at the same time more animal than we might like and less godlike than we might hope, this meditation on our unique universal predicament seeks in evolution's parable a guide to discovering the balance between the wisdom of animals and the arrogance of gods.

ENVIRONMENTAL POLITICS:

Rachel Carson; *Silent Spring*; Houghton Mifflin, 1987 (twenty-fifth anniversary edition).

Rachel Carson was fifty years old and a well-known nature writer when she began writing Silent Spring in 1958. First published in 1962, this book in many senses created the post-World War II environmental movement, with its clear teachings about the chemical destruction of the environment by pesticides, especially DDT. *Silent Spring* was a clarion call about "the basic irresponsibility of an industrialized, technological society toward the natural world," in the words of Paul Brooks, editor of this edition and biographer of Rachel Carson. Perhaps some indication of its truth and power can be gained from the vehemence of the chemical industry's response, which was to attempt to halt publication and, when that failed, to spend hundreds of thousands of dollars to discredit the book and malign its author as an "ignorant and hysterical" woman (she was actually a well-trained scientist). *Silent Spring*'s message and sensitivity are still salient today, still sobering, especially considering how little has changed in the 25 years since its publication.

John Elkington, Julia Hailes and Joel Makower; *The Green Consumer*; Penguin, 1990.

The Green Consumer is one of the most comprehensive guides for consumers who want to "green" their shopping. It will help you identify products with less (or no) packaging, made from recycled materials, free of ozone-depleting chemicals, and so on. Each product category comes with a general discussion of the environmental issues related to it — all in all, a very informative and helpful resource. Also *The Green Consumer Letter*, a monthly newsletter tracking developments relating to the environmental aspects of products. More up-to-date than the book. Available from Tilden Press, 1526 Connecticut Avenue, NW, Washington, DC 20036; (202) 332-1700.

Debra Lynn Dadd; *Nontoxic, Natural and Earthwise*; Jeremy P. Tarcher, Inc., 1990.

This is another excellent book for consumers trying to distinguish real green products from the pretenders. Using five criteria — ingredients, packaging, energy use, compassion to animals, and social responsibility — Dadd reviews hundreds of brand name products. In addition, she offers a list at the end of the book of mail-order houses, which is sometimes the only place you can currently find alternatives not available in "mainstream" stores.

Henry Hobhouse; *Seeds of Change: Five Plants That Transformed Mankind*; Harper & Row, 1987.

Similar to the above book, but with perhaps more political "bite." Looking at our intertwined history with quinine, sugar cane, tea, cotton and the potato, Henry Hobhouse draws a compelling and ingenious portrait of just how connected we are with the natural world. A sometimes amusing, always fascinating answer to humankind's arrogant insistence on autonomy from nature, we see exactly how "a bunch of plants" helped shape the fates of people and nations.

Christopher Manes; *Green Rage: Radical Environmentalism and the Unmaking of Civilization*; Little, Brown & Co., 1990.

Powerful, cogent and wonderfully straightforward, this book details the rise of the radical environmental movement, best known perhaps by the group Earth First! Reading Manes' polemical account will reveal why those who care about the fate of the Earth felt driven to civil disobedience in order to halt the depredations of industrial and consumer society. The stories of sell-outs by mainstream environmental organizations, of compromises that led to more wilderness destruction, will make you angry and sad. Hopefully, readers will also understand better how "deep ecology" is maligned by those who accuse it of misanthropy.

Susan Meeker-Lowry; *Economics As If The Earth Really Mattered*; New Society Publishers, 1986.

Long active in seeking to change corporate behavior, Meeker-Lowry gathers here her accumulated wisdom on nothing less than how to create a new ethical economics. Full of examples, this is a well-written manual which covers everything from socially responsible investing to corporate boycotts to small-scale community entrepreneurship.

Charles Piller; *The Fail-Safe Society: Community Defiance and the End of American Technological Optimism*; Basic Books, 1991.

Charles Piller was probably like most people in his attitudes toward the NIMBY mentality (Not In My Back Yard). He set out to write a book that showed NIMBY groups to be yet another sign of American know-nothingism: community selfishness, technophobia, and so on. What he discovered instead (and the reader will too hopefully), through a study of three very different campaigns, is that most allegedly NIMBY protests are a response to decades of disinformation from scientific "experts," failures of corporate technology, and condescension to (if not outright dismissal of) local feelings. A thorough, illuminating and necessary read.

Andrew Revkin; *The Burning Season: the Murder of Chico Mendes and the Fight for the Amazon Rain Forest*; Houghton Mifflin Company, 1990.

The tale of the Amazon's destruction as told through the harassment and murder of Chico Mendes, rubbertapper, union leader and self-taught environmental activist. This tremendously sad story is engagingly and movingly told by Andrew Revkin, who is himself a well-known science journalist.

Works Cited

Abram, David. "The Perceptual Implications of Gaia." *The Ecologist*. Ecosystems Ltd., U.K.: Vol.15, No. 3, 1987.

Berry, Wendell. *A Continuous Harmony*. New York: Harcourt Brace Jovanovich, 1970.
    Excerpts from *A Continuous Harmony: Essays Cultural and Agricultural,* copyright © 1972 by Wendell Berry, reprinted by permission of Harcourt Brace Jovanovich, Inc.

Berry, Wendell. *The Gift of Good Land*. San Francisco: North Point Press, 1981.

Buber, Martin, *I and Thou*. Translated by Walter Kaufmann. New York: Charles Scribner's Sons, 1970.
    Reprinted with the permission of Charles Scribner's Sons, an imprint of MacMillan Publishing Company from *I and Thou* by Martin Buber, translated by Walter Kaufmann. Translation copyright © 1970 by Charles Scribner's Sons.

Carson, Rachel. *Silent Spring*. Greenwich, Connecticut: Fawcett Publications, 1962.

Dillard, Annie. *Pilgrim at Tinker Creek*. New York: Bantam Books, 1974.
    Copyright © 1974 by Annie Dillard. Excerpt from *Pilgrim at Tinker Creek* reprinted by permission of HarperCollins.

The Fathers According to Rabbi Nathan. Translated by Judah Goldin. New Haven: Yale University Press, copyright © 1955.

Goldberg, Natalie. *Writing Down the Bones*. Boston: Shambala, 1986.

Heschel, Abraham Joshua. *God in Search of Man*. New York: Farrar, Straus & Cudahy, 1955.
Heschel, Abraham, Joshua, *The Sabbath*. New York: Farrar, Straus and Giroux, 1951.
    Excerpts from *God in Search of Man* by Abraham Joshua Heschel. Copyright © 1955 by Abraham Joshua Heschel. Copyright renewed © 1983 by Sylvia Heschel. Reprinted by permission of Farrar, Straus & Giroux, Inc.. Excerpt from *The Sabbath* by Abraham Joshua Heschel. Copyright © 1951 by Abraham Joshua Heschel. Copyright renewed © 1979 by Sylvia Heschel. Reprinted by permission of Farrar, Straus & Giroux, Inc.

Hirsch, S.R. *Horeb: A Philosophy of Jewish Law*. Translated by Dr. I Grunfeld. New York: Soncino, 1975.

Hirsch, S.R. *The Nineteen Letters of Ben Uzziel*. Translated by Rabbi Bernard Drachman. Prepared by Jacob Breuer. New York: Feldheim Press, 1969.

Ibn Ezra, Abraham. "God Everywhere." Translated by D.E. de L. *An Anthology of Medieval Hebrew Literature*. Edited by Abraham E. Milgrom. New York: The Burning Bush Press,1961.

Ibn Pakuda, Bahya. *Duties of the Heart*. Translated by Moses Hyamson. New York: Feldheim, 1970.

Kaplan, Mordechai, M. *Judaism as Civilization*. New York: MacMillan, 1934.

Klagsbrun, Francine. *Voices of Wisdom: Jewish Ideals and Ethics for Everyday Living*. New York: Pantheon Books, 1980.

Kushner, Lawrence. *The Book of Miracles*. New York: UAHC Press, 1987.

Leopold, Aldo. *A Sand County Almanac*. New York: Ballantine, 1989.
    A Sand County Almanac by Aldo Leopold. Copyright © 1949 by Oxford University Press, Inc.

Lovelock, James, *Gaia: A New Look at Life on Earth*. Oxford: Oxford University Press,1979.
    Reprinted with permission of Oxford University Press, Oxford, U.K.

Maimonides, Moses. *Guide of the Perplexed*. Translated by M. Friedlander. New York: Hebrew Publishing Company, 1881.

Maimonides, Moses. *The Preservation of Youth: The Guide to Health*. Translated by Hirsch L. Gordon. New York: Philosophical Library, 1958.

Maimonides, Moses. *The Book of Judges*. Translated by Abraham Hirschman. New Haven: Yale University Press, 1949.

Nelson, Richard, *The Island Within*. New York: Vintage Books, 1991.
    From "The Forest of the Eyes" in *The Island Within*. Copyright © 1989 by Richard Nelson. Published in the United States by Vintage Books, a division of Random House, Inc. New York. Originally published in hardcover by North Point Press, California, 1989. Reprinted by permission of Susan Bergholz Literary Services.

Neihardt, John G. *Black Elk Speaks*. Omaha: University of Nebraska Press,1961.
    Reprinted from *Black Elk Speaks* by John G. Neihardt, permission of the University of Nebraska Press. Copyright © 1932, 1959, 1972, by John G. Neihardt. Copyright © 1961 by the John G. Neihardt Trust.

50 Simple Things You Can Do To Save The Earth. Berkley, California: Earthworks Press, 1989.

Rifkin, Jeremy. Interview. *Whole Earth Review*. Sausalito, California: Point Foundation, Winter, 1988.

Roberts, Warren and Harry T. Moore. Ed.s. "A Propos of Lady Chatterly's Lover". *Phoenix II: Uncollected, Unpublished, and Other Prose Works by D.H. Lawrence.* New York:The Viking Press, 1968.

> "A Propos of LADY CHATTERLEY'S LOVER", copyright 1930 by Frieda Lawrence, renewed © 1958 by the Estate of Frieda Lawrence Ravagli, from PHEONIX II: THE POSTHUMOUS PAPERS OF D.H. LAWRENCE by D.H. Lawrence, edited by Roberts and Moore. Used by permission of Viking Penguin, a division of Penguin Books USA Inc.

"Everything's Broken" by Bob Dylan. Copyright © 1989 by Special Rider Music. All rights reserved, used by permission.

TURN! TURN! TURN! (To Everything There Is A Season) Words from the Book of Ecclesiastes, adaptation and music by Pete Seeger. Copyright © 1962 (renewed) by Melody Trails, Inc. New York, NY.

For Further Reading

Berger, John. *Restoring the Earth*. New York: Doubleday, 1987

Berry, Thomas. *The Dream of the Earth*, San Francisco: Sierra Book Club, 1988.

Berry, Wendell. *Home Economics*. San Francisco: North Point Press, 1987.

Eisley, Loren. *The Immense Journey*. New York: Vintage Books, 1959.

Encyclopedia Judaica, Volume 3, New York: Keter Publishing Company, 1973.

Finch, Robert and Jon Elder. Eds. *The Norton Book of Nature Writing*. New York: W.W. Norton Company, 1990

Goldfarb, Theodore D. *Taking Sides: Clashing Views on Controversial Environmental Issues*. Guilford, Ct.: Dushkin Publishing Group, 1989.

Gould, Stephen Jay. *Time's Arrow, Time's Cycle: Myth and Metaphor in the Discovery of Geological Time*. Cambridge, Mass.:Harvard University Press, 1987.

Lipkis, Andy and Katie. *The Simple Act of Planting a Tree: Healing Your Neighborhood, Your City, and Your World*. Los Angeles, Ca.: Jeremy P. Tarcher, Inc., 1990.

Margolin, Malcolm. *The Earth Manual*. Berkeley: Heyday Books, 1975.

Miller, Avigdor. *Rejoice O Youth*, Brooklyn, New York: Balshon Printing, 1962.

Nabhan, Gary. *The Desert Smells Like Rain*. San Francisco: North Point Press, 1987.

Nash, Roderick Frazier. *The Right of Nature: A History of Environmenta Ethics*. Madison, Wisconsin: University of Wisconsin Press, 1989.

The Essential Whole Earth Catalogue. Point Foundation, New York: Doubleday & Co., 1986.

Siegal, Richard, Michael Strassfeld, Sharon Strassfeld. *The First Jewish Catalogue*. Philadelphia: The Jewish Publication Society, 1973.

Srassfeld, Michael. *The Jewish Holidays*. New York: Harper and Row, 1985.

Stevens, Peter, *Design With Nature*. Boston: Atlantic Monthly Press, 1974.

Thomas, Lewis, *Lives of A Cell*, Toronto: Bantam Books, 1974

Thompson, Darcy, *On Growth and Form*. Cambridge: Cambridge University Press, Cambridge, 1961

Tobias, Michael. Ed. *Deep Ecology*. San Diego: Avant Books, 1985.

Wallace, David Rains. *The Klamath Knot*. San Francisco: Sierra Club Books, 1984.

Waskow, Arthur. *Seasons of Our Joy*. New York: Summit Books, 1982.